Stay Together or Break Up?

Codependency in Relationships

How to Identify and Overcome a Toxic Partnership
Discover Your Journey to Emotional, Self-Determined
Freedom and True Self-Love

MARIA REED

© **Copyright 2023 - All rights reserved.**

The content contained within this book may not be reproduced, duplicated or transmitted without direct written permission from the author or the publisher.

Under no circumstances will any blame or legal responsibility be held against the publisher, or author, for any damages, reparation, or monetary loss due to the information contained within this book. Either directly or indirectly. You are responsible for your own choices, actions, and results.

Legal Notice:

This book is copyright protected. This book is only for personal use. You cannot amend, distribute, sell, use, quote or paraphrase any part, or the content within this book, without the consent of the author or publisher.

Disclaimer Notice:

Please note the information contained within this document is for educational and entertainment purposes only. All effort has been executed to present accurate, up to date, and reliable, complete information. No warranties of any kind are declared or implied. Readers acknowledge that the author is not engaging in the rendering of legal, financial, medical or professional advice. The content within this book has been derived from various sources. Please consult a licensed professional before attempting any techniques outlined in this book.

By reading this document, the reader agrees that under no circumstances is the author responsible for any losses, direct or indirect, which are incurred as a result of the use of the information contained within this document, including, but not limited to, — errors, omissions, or inaccuracies.

Table of Contents

Introduction 5

Chapter 1: What is Codependency? 7
   Definition 7
   Types of Dependency 9
   Who is Prone to Codependency? 29

Chapter 2: How Does Codependency Develop? 37
   Background 37
   Hidden Goals 42
   Needs Behind Codependency 46

Chapter 3: Living in Codependence 55

Chapter 4: Codependence in Relationships 95

Chapter 5: Breaking Free from Codependence 105
   The Main Fears of Codependents in the
   Healing Process 107
   What is the Right Thing to Do? 112
   What Do I Really Want? 116
   Who am I? 120
   Out of False Hope and Into Faith 123
   Out of Credulity and into Trust 125
   Out of Altruism and into Genuine Devotion 127

"Wise Advice"..129
Completion – When the Dependent
Individual Becomes Unrecognizable..........................130

Conclusion **133**

Resources and Further Reading..............................**135**

Introduction

Welcome, dear reader!

This book delves into a subject that explores the depths of human longing and its entanglements. Codependency is a state that we often find ourselves in without fully realizing it and breaking free from it can seem challenging as we strive for a more fulfilling and relieving reality.

However, the more we delve into understanding how dependency arises, what our true longings are, and the value that such experiences can bring, the more we can learn, gain strength, and cultivate self-confidence. Our challenges, though they may initially feel like stumbling blocks, also present us with opportunities. Therefore, this book aims to encourage you to uncover the treasures within difficult phases of life and transform your pain into triumph.

Addictions carry a heavy burden, leaving individuals feeling powerless, frustrated, and often consumed by anger and despair. It is crucial to delve deeper and uncover the dynamics behind these emotions and sobering experiences.

This book is for you if:

- You wish to explore the topic of codependency in general.
- You are in a codependent relationship and seeking a way out.
- You fear that the path to freedom may require sacrificing everything and find the journey daunting.
- You wish to provide support and encouragement to someone caught in a codependent situation.
- You refuse to allow the challenges to drag you deeper into a downward spiral and instead view them as valuable experiences for personal growth.
- You sense that a codependent situation is holding your potential captive, and you yearn for freedom.
- You seek a hopeful, empathetic, and non-judgmental space as you read.
- You desire practical tips and self-help resources.

People in desperate circumstances are in great need of hope. Therefore, this book aims to empower you, tap into your self-efficacy, guide you toward letting go of love, discover a new purpose, and find solace in the care of your loved ones. Genuine help lies in understanding the inner struggles of all those involved and offering a pathway that can be followed by anyone seeking a solution.

Chapter 1
What is Codependency?

"Bondage is hoarse, and may not speak aloud."

William Shakespeare

Definition

Codependency refers to a dependent relationship and entanglement with a person who is addicted, emotionally distressed, or otherwise in personal dependency. In such relationships, one's own needs and goals are often abandoned or pushed to the background, prioritizing the care of the person struggling with dependency. Codependency is also present when an individual's own life and well-being heavily rely on the choices, lifestyle, emotional landscape, and charisma of another person due to this entanglement.

In essence, the codependent individual is trapped within their own emotional landscape and life design, repeatedly adapting their behavior to meet the needs and expectations of their loved one. By intertwining their life with the other person's and making their own freedom contingent upon it, the codependent inadvertently reinforces addictive behaviors, hinders personal responsibility on the part of the loved one, and perpetuates an enmeshed connection, further solidifying unhealthy patterns.

Many codependents feel compelled to be considerate and show great understanding, sacrifice, and forbearance in order to support their loved ones and make them feel less alone. They assume responsibility for providing time, energy, and assistance on a daily basis, in the hopes of facilitating positive change in the other person's life. However, this devotion to the dependent individuals pulls them into a downward spiral, driven by their strong emotional attachment and fear of losing the person in question. This dynamic reveals that codependents themselves possess addictive structures that draw them away from their own needs and lead them to project those needs onto others. In contrast, the dependent is typically self-absorbed, consciously or unconsciously using the codependent as a means to maintain a certain stability that they cannot find within themselves.

Codependency is dangerous because it involves surrendering one's self-efficacy and responsibility for personal well-being to someone who is incapable of reciprocating. The energy directed towards the dependent individuals never returns in a nourishing manner. Instead, it manifests as highly charged energy, resulting in conflicts, intense emotions, contentious entanglements, and accusations. The draining nature of codependency can also manifest through unhealthy silence, defensiveness, passivity, and emotional barriers, which may be more difficult to recognize.

Many individuals struggling with dependency are drawn to codependent relationships because they themselves do not maintain a healthy attitude toward themselves and others. The loved ones of individuals are driven by the persistent hope that their love and support will eventually lead them to reconsider their behavior and break free from their bondage. They aspire to motivate and, perhaps, even become the catalyst for the dependent individual's self-awareness and liberation from their destructive habits, all out of love for their loved one.

Deep within the codependent individual lies a longing for self-worth and the desire to be significant enough for someone to make positive choices out of love for them. They lack the self-esteem necessary to create a healthy and nurturing relationship environment on their own.

Types of Dependency

People can become codependent in any situation where they are associated with someone who is themselves dependent. Dependency is evident in addictions such as alcoholism, drug addiction, and other material substances. However, any form of substitute gratification can lead to addiction, and individuals connected to someone dependent on substances can become codependent under certain circumstances. Emotional addictions also fall within the realm of bondage and can contribute to codependent relationships. The inability or refusal to confront inner growth and take responsibility for one's own decisions affects those in close proximity and fosters codependency.

The following are some of the most common manifestations of codependency.

Addiction

Alcohol and drug addiction often foster codependent relationships. Many individuals dependent on substances rely on a social network or a specific partner who provides them with stability, closeness, and social support. In doing so, they transfer their responsibility to the willing codependent, who, driven by the hope of a positive outcome, invests their time, energy, money, and emotional support.

All forms of addiction are a plea for freedom, connection, and happiness. Codependents perceive and empathize with the vulnerable and needy side of the person with addiction, often drawing from their own experiences of pain and longing. They possess a high level of empathy and sensitivity towards the needs of others. However, their empathetic nature sometimes takes precedence over their own self-worth and conflicts with their desire to lead fulfilling lives.

Codependent partners and relatives tend to shower the dependent individual with empathy and compassion, often enabling their behavior instead of setting boundaries. Unconsciously, they reinforce the dependent individual's tendency to make excuses and perpetuate the role of the helpless victim. It is not uncommon for codependents to be accused of being uncharitable and harsh when they try to say no or withdraw their support.

Any form of drug addiction represents an escape from personal responsibility and a retreat from the realities of life. Individuals struggling with dependency find their fears, anxieties, unmet needs, and painful traumatic experiences overwhelming. They use drugs to suppress feelings of shame, helplessness, powerlessness, pain from loss, failure, and inadequacy. Drugs also represent a yearning for a sense of aliveness, wholeness, and connectedness.

Codependency develops when:

- The person with addiction does not seek help and remains passive.
- The person with addiction expects their loved ones to carry them.
- The codependent fails to establish boundaries and acts and communicates inconsistently.
- Common obligations, family structures, and possessions bind the individuals together.
- Manipulation and violence dominate the relationship.
- Empathy is mistaken for self-sacrifice.

Matthias has been struggling with alcohol addiction for three years and appears to be making a positive change, at least on the surface. In reality, he refuses to seek help and succumbs to his addiction without restraint, frequently getting drunk to the point of unconsciousness. His living space is chaotic, and he hides behind his computer screen.

When Matthias meets the attractive Sabrina, who is immediately charmed by him, he downplays his addiction. He claims to be undergoing treatment and experiencing initial success. Sabrina is impressed by his supposed honesty and open confession about his condition, and she decides to join Matthias on his path to recovery. She believes Matthias has taken responsibility and convinces herself that her presence will further motivate him.

The two fall in love, spending exciting nights together, and Sabrina starts visiting Matthias more frequently. She ignores the fact that his living space is becoming increasingly chaotic and cluttered. In recent years, Sabrina's own life has felt dull and uneventful, so she welcomes the opportunity to expand her horizons, as she confides in a friend.

Matthias does attend a few meetings with a social worker and appears to be making progress. However, he continues to drink, albeit appearing cheerful and hopeful in Sabrina's presence. As a result, Sabrina becomes more deeply involved with Matthias and admires his motivation.

Eventually, Sabrina allows Matthias to move in with her, believing that a loving and orderly environment will provide him with the opportunity to change. However, once he settles in, his true nature emerges. Matthias becomes even more intoxicated than before and, after a few weeks, destroys their bedroom in a fit of rage. Startled from her idealized vision of a life together, Sabrina realizes that she had overlooked many red flags: Matthias' smug grin when he gains the upper hand in an argument, beer bottles accumulating in the trash can, his perpetually glazed eyes, and canceled appointments with the social worker, often accompanied by excuses like "I want to work on a job application" or "I'm not feeling well today" or "I want to help you in the garden."

Sabrina must confront the fact that she is codependent. She became involved with Matthias out of a longing for adventure, only to find herself being exploited by him as a means of escape from his own struggles.

Narcissism

> *"The facade is deceptive: In truth, narcissists harbor the feeling of being unable to meet the demands placed upon them. Insults such as job loss or breakups frequently trigger profound emotional crises."*
>
> Marian Grosser

Narcissism is a domain where codependency predominantly occurs on an emotional level. Narcissistic individuals possess a magnetic ability to attract empathic and highly sensitive people who willingly conform to them and revolve around them.

Narcissism is characterized by the following traits:

- Exaggerated and superficial self-confidence, with sufferers holding an excessively high opinion of themselves.
- Power fantasies, a craving for success, and an addiction to admiration.
- Lack of empathy.
- Everything is related to themselves, and they exhibit selfish behaviors, taking advantage of others.

- Difficulty in handling criticism.
- Rejection of healthy self-reflection, with sufferers expecting everything to revolve around them.
- Patterns of action that can be choleric, silent, or manipulative, putting others under pressure, making them dependent, or inducing guilt.

Codependency with a narcissist arises from the narcissist's obsession with excessive self-centeredness. The narcissist becomes addicted to the admiration of others and continuously focuses on their own perceived grandeur, driven by a deep sense of inferiority.

Affected codependents often fall deeply and passionately in love with a narcissist, initially seeing qualities in them that they feel are lacking in themselves, such as interesting thoughts, self-confidence, a firm standpoint, assertiveness, charisma, and charm. Many codependents idealize the narcissist, placing them on a pedestal and excessively admiring them. As a result, their attention becomes solely focused on the narcissist, providing the ideal breeding ground for the narcissist's addiction to admiration. In this process, the codependent is used for the narcissist's well-being, while losing touch with their own inner center.

Codependency with narcissists can lead to severe mental breakdowns, exhaustion, loss of self-perception, and distortion of gut feelings. Narcissists often distort the truth, blame, and shame the codependent, keeping them in a submissive position. The codependent is labeled as empathic, cold, and unloving as soon as they express frustration or anger for not receiving attention in the relationship. Their needs are deemed less important, with the narcissist's problems always taking precedence. Consequently, the codependent sacrifices themselves for the other's sake and frequently ends up in burnout, shadowing the narcissist in their everyday life.

Narcissism and codependency manifest not only in romantic relationships but also in parent-child dynamics (when one parent is narcissistic, and the child lacks the opportunity for autonomous development). Furthermore, they can be observed in larger organized groups within companies, politics, or even in religious and spiritual settings.

Example:

Linda had a deep affection for her church community. Every Sunday, she faithfully attended church and dedicated herself to serving the church - or rather, serving the pastor. The pastor had a captivating presence and could sway the entire congregation with just a few sentences. His words were filled with charisma and passion, his gestures were moving, and his aura exuded both a fatherly and an exciting masculine energy. When the pastor fervently called for donations to the church, the collection bag would be filled with hundreds of dollars. Many members, following the pastor's advice, donated ten percent of their income each month, firmly believing that they were pleasing God in this manner.

Codependency in Relationships

Linda was among the generous contributors. She was fascinated by the pastor's passionate and charismatic demeanor, feeling a strong desire to be close to him. She attributed this longing to the vitality that God seemed to bestow upon the pastor. Despite not earning much herself, Linda would often sacrifice everything she had, driven by the aspiration to make the pastor proud. She actively participated in church activities, sang in the choir on Sundays, and found a sense of belonging within the church community.

However, after a few months as a churchgoer, Linda began experiencing increasing frustration. When the pastor became too occupied to pay attention to her, she felt drained and weary. While he frequently praised her dedication and faith in the shared vision, making Linda feel particularly chosen, she started to grow skeptical. During his sermons, the pastor often used himself as an example to promote a godly lifestyle, emphasizing the significance of his own ministry.

Linda's doubts intensified when she noticed that only about half of the parishioners attended the service whenever the pastor announced his absence. Could it be right for the worship service to be so dependent on one person? Shouldn't every parishioner be valued and able to cultivate their own spiritual relationship without constantly idolizing the pastor? Moreover, she wondered why more and more people were withdrawing and leaving the church community, often labeled as rebellious and non-conforming in secret. The pastor's reaction was striking: he spoke ill of the "apostates" behind their backs, portraying them as individuals who had turned their backs on God by leaving this particular church community. He believed that his way of practicing spirituality was the standard above all other options and criticized many members for their perceived immaturity, urging them to seek his counsel more often.

Years later, as Linda reflects on that period, she shares her perspective:

"It wasn't God who bestowed such charisma upon our pastor. It was his grandiosity, his belief that he was the embodiment of the church, the exemplary Christian, the leader who held the members in check. I realized too late how mesmerized everyone was by him during his sermons, and even in my personal life, I would spend hours talking and thinking about him with my partner throughout the week. My actions were intertwined with him. Even when faced with a personal decision, I would ponder what he would think about it. When I finally became aware of what was happening, it was almost too late. I started questioning things, no longer accepting everything that was dictated. Immediately, I was branded as a rebel and shunned. The pastor went as far as accusing me of no longer loving God when I withdrew my admiration and refused to let his judgment dominate my life. When I stopped giving regular donations, he took it personally. At times, I felt terrible, like a black sheep who had betrayed their family. It eventually led to burnout, and only with the help of therapy did I manage to break free from the church community."

Like Linda, many codependents find themselves entangled in narcissistic relationships. They lose confidence in themselves and their ability to make their own decisions. They start doubting their own perspective and may even reconsider their life plans due to the influence of the narcissist. Some become so consumed by their narcissistic partner or influencer that they no longer have any space to shape their own lives. They feel compelled to prioritize the needs and problems of the narcissist over their own.

Narcissism is primarily characterized by the absence of space for anyone else besides the narcissist. A woman who ended her relationship with a narcissistic partner after becoming pregnant and having an abortion said, "You cannot live with a person like that." She made the decision to leave before becoming dependent on his delusions of grandeur and losing herself in the process.

Abuse

Codependency resulting from abuse is one of the most manipulative and violent areas within the realm of addiction. Abuse can manifest on physical, emotional, and psychological levels, and it can be carried out by individuals who are addicted to power, control, intense emotions, or various substances. Codependency occurs when the abused person becomes trapped in this dynamic and is unable to break free or even recognize the extent of the abuse. Due to the severity of this issue, it is important to seek professional help and support. If you find yourself in a codependent relationship with someone who exerts power, control, and violence over you and who is also struggling with addiction or the need for power, it is strongly recommended that you reach out for assistance. At the end of this book, you will find a list of resources and organizations that can provide help.

Self-Destructive Behavior

Self-destructive behavior encompasses disorders such as anorexia, bulimia, self-harm, and other forms of self-injury. Self-destructive behavior often stems from deep psychological or physical wounds, traumatic experiences, and serious medical conditions, all of which require professional help and support. However, it is still important to address this topic and provide some important insights, as even small-scale self-destructive behaviors can have a significant negative impact on relationships and can lead to codependency.

Individuals who suffer from anorexia, bulimia, or other self-destructive behaviors often become intensely focused on their own pain. The addiction takes control of their lives and dictates their daily existence. Those who live with individuals struggling with such behaviors may become codependent as they sympathize deeply or feel compelled to support them. They may hope to regulate their eating behaviors, soften the impact of their attacks, coax them into recovery, or provide structure, security, and reliability in an effort to free them from their addiction. Many codependents express a belief that they must be constantly present to prevent the affected person from succumbing to their addictive behaviors when they are alone. They exhaust all their strength and energy in protecting the individuals with self-destructive behaviors from themselves. Often, they are driven by an overwhelming fear of losing the person and bearing the weight of responsibility for their actions, becoming deeply entangled in the complexities of codependency.

Sabrina deeply loves her younger sister, Mona, who suffers from severe bulimia. Mona consistently turns to her older sister, placing her trust in their unbreakable bond. "It's the two of us against the world," they often say. The sisters live together in an apartment, and Sabrina harbors anxiety whenever she has to leave Mona alone. She struggles to find peace during those moments.

Sabrina increasingly feels burdened by the immense responsibility of safeguarding her sister. She catches herself yearning for freedom, longing to focus more on her own needs, and even contemplating moving out of their shared apartment. However, overwhelming guilt plagues her thoughts, as Mona lacks a stable social network to rely on.

As a child, Sabrina assumed the internal responsibility for Mona's well-being. With emotionally absent parents, Sabrina adopted a nurturing mother role, which she has continued to fulfill ever since. When she successfully prevents Mona from experiencing a binge episode, she feels needed and proud. Yet, if she is unable to help, she is consumed by feelings of inadequacy and shame. This internal drive reinforces codependency and keeps Sabrina trapped in an entangled web.

Self-Sabotage

Self-sabotage is a result of inner beliefs that question one's own worth and self-efficacy. It often occurs when individuals are afraid to move forward:

- I am afraid that if I let go of my victim mindset, no one will pay attention to me, so I must always feel bad.
- I am afraid of failure, so I refuse to accept challenges.

- I am afraid to open up in a love relationship, so I remain closed and dismissive towards my partner.
- I am afraid of not receiving care once I am well, so I stay stuck in a state of sickness.
- I fear anything new because it makes me vulnerable, so I sabotage my own growth.

Those who are codependent with someone who engages in self-sabotage allow their own growth to be hindered, limited, and stifled by the relentless self-destructive patterns of the self-saboteur. In this dynamic, codependents often complain that the self-saboteur clings to them and yet refuses to cooperate in building a life together. Self-saboteurs often feel justified in their actions because their internal patterns tell them that they must play the role of the loser, the victim, or the loner. They feel worthless, pursued by bad luck, or destined to be solitary - and they find their identity within these beliefs.

Manuel is a talented musician with an impressive voice. However, he is severely overweight, chronically ill with asthma, and repeatedly experiences failed relationships. While performing on the street, he attracts a crowd of people who admire his talent. But as soon as he engages in conversation, he diminishes himself to the point where people quickly withdraw:

"I won't be able to perform next week, it's going to be too hot, my illness is acting up... I hope I can come back soon. My voice may be good, but women only want my talent, not me. I'm so unattractive... How can anyone overlook that?"

Codependency in Relationships

There seems to be a pull within Manuel, constantly needing words of encouragement and validation to keep him going. At the same time, an internal program compels him to lean back in satisfaction only when he receives the expected rejection. Self-sabotage keeps Manuel in a victim posture, shielding him from the deep fear of actual rejection if he were to let his own light shine fully.

One day, he meets a young woman who exudes empathy and independence. Manuel's talent moves her, and they become friends. The young woman showers Manuel with encouragement and consistently holds a positive view of him. Secretly, Manuel falls in love with her - or rather, with the energy she gives him. Yet, he already suspects that he cannot win her over, so he preemptively rejects all compliments and criticizes himself. The young woman feels increasingly drained and exhausted after each encounter. She feels the need to give more and more to uplift and validate Manuel further. Over time, her desire wanes, and she experiences frustration. She becomes angry that her compliments seem to dissolve within the depths of Manuel's low self-esteem. Despite her awareness that this situation may never change, she holds on, driven by a faint hope that Manuel will one day recognize his worth and begin to shine. She justifies her attachment by saying she always seeks and highlights the gold in others, hoping that her positive influence will ignite a healthy sense of self-worth in Manuel. Only later does she realize that she is emotionally codependent on Manuel's self-sabotaging behavior, constantly yearning for him to become the ideal partner she longs for. She saw something in Manuel that attracted her and attempted to bolster his self-esteem in the hope of building a loving relationship.

In essence, this woman is unaware of her own value. She believes that she must change others in order to be desired instead of seeking someone within herself who is capable of offering love and affection. In her inner world, the possibility of being desired and wanted by an emotionally stable individual does not even register - she only feels secure and empowered when reflected in the presence of someone she perceives as having lower self-worth. In the presence of emotionally stable individuals, she feels small and empty.

She hides this deep fear behind a façade of selflessness and a moral code of always being encouraging and empowering to others - constantly searching for the good in them. However, the truth lies in latent codependency stemming from her own low self-esteem.

Inferiority Complex

An inferiority complex can drive partners and loved ones into codependency. This entanglement develops when the person suffering from the inferiority complex constantly relies on others to feel good about themselves. They exploit the other person's closeness, attention, and devotion to keep themselves afloat. The inferiority complex can be closely linked to narcissistic tendencies, but it can also stem from a refusal to grow, deep-seated fears, intense shame, or other internal blockages that intensify feelings of inferiority and impact all relationships. This often results in a one-sided dynamic where the person with the inferiority complex takes rather than gives. It can also manifest as a permanent victim mentality. The field is broad, and a sense of inferiority lurks beneath nearly every emotional weakness. To illustrate this section, we will focus on the feeling of inferiority that manifests as a fear of rejection.

Individuals who feel excessively insecure about themselves often display demanding behaviors or exhibit passivity in relationships. In such cases, a partner or family member who is also emotionally insecure can fall into codependent patterns by constantly trying to alleviate the other person's suffering. They may diminish themselves to avoid making the insecure person feel bad or consistently sacrifice their own life plans and authentic self to avoid surprising or rejecting the anxious individual. The dependent person's negative self-perception, which hinges on the attention of others, becomes the responsibility of the codependent person, who tries to convey a sense of worth to the dependent individual.

Claudia always yearned for a partner who would worship her and make her the center of their world. She believed she had found such a relationship with Marco, but it turned out differently than she had envisioned. For Marco, Claudia is his dream woman, and he considers himself fortunate to be with her. However, the scales are imbalanced. Marco is dependent on Claudia's validation. Deep down, he feels it is too good to be true that a woman like her would choose someone like him. He suffers from a strong sense of inferiority and firmly believes he is unworthy of her love. As a result, he places Claudia on a pedestal and almost idolizes her.

Claudia experiences conflicting emotions in this situation. On one hand, she enjoys being adored. On the other hand, she soon realizes that Marco's love feels like a golden cage. He is quick to take offense, becomes easily displeased, and displays anger, implying that she doesn't give him enough attention. Although Marco tries to hide his anger, it permeates every interaction between them. Claudia senses a cloud of expectations and feels compelled to continually provide attention and affection, which seemingly disappears into a black hole with Marco—her efforts never seem enough. However, she doesn't want to hurt Marco and continues striving to maintain the image of being the perfect dream woman for him. This places her under immense pressure.

Claudia also senses that Marco is highly unsettled not only by a lack of attention but also by any inconsistencies in her character and behavior. Whenever Claudia is in a bad mood or feels insecure, Marco becomes nervous, fearing abandonment. Thus, he can only relax when Claudia is consistently friendly, loving, and radiant towards him. He needs an idol to lean on. Through his devotion and sacrifices, he keeps Claudia attached to him. It takes a long time for her to admit that this kind of devotion is not what she has truly longed for. Claudia finds herself in a codependent relationship with a man who cannot stand on his own. She has to take care of his emotional well-being and keep his anxiety at bay. In the process, she deprives herself of the opportunity to simply be human and to be loved for who she truly is. She has become a projection surface and does not immediately sever this connection because she is also driven by fear—the fear of not being loved and not being interesting enough for self-assured, emotionally strong men.

Unresolved Past and Entanglements

All individuals carry unresolved aspects from their past into their relationships. It is a normal human experience, as no one is perfect or completely whole in this sense. However, if we fail to take responsibility for these old burdens and let go of them, we burden our environment, and codependency can arise, even if it is unintentional. A particularly illustrative example of holding onto past love demonstrates this:

Nadine sought refuge in a new relationship after a grueling long-term affair. Her new partner, Michael, is emotionally available, attentive, and committed. However, Nadine can't seem to forget about her previous affair. She longs for her ex-partner both physically and emotionally, which puts an enormous strain on her new relationship. Michael, being a romantic at heart, has learned from his past to patiently wait for love. He enters the relationship with Nadine without setting boundaries and clearly communicating that he wants her to be emotionally available for him. He places himself on an emotional waiting bench, devotedly trying to win Nadine's heart. He does everything he can to convince her to let go of the past.

But Nadine is not ready to take responsibility for this process. As a result, Michael falls into codependency due to his lack of boundaries. He cannot grow in a mature, healthy relationship because he expects something from Nadine that she is unable to give. He has chosen Nadine, someone who reinforces his unconscious belief that he is not worthy enough to be fully chosen. The codependency becomes evident in his constant efforts to take responsibility for Nadine's emotional well-being and persuade her.

Depression

Depression can manifest as temporary moodiness, but it can also be a long-term clinical diagnosis. The following section focuses on the latter.

Partners, children, and loved ones of individuals with depression often find themselves in codependent relationships. They face a challenging predicament because they want to be there for their loved ones and provide support. However, depression often persists, making their efforts seem futile. The cloud of depression not only dampens the affected individual's zest for life but also affects the moods of those around them, causing codependents to suffer greatly. Particularly empathetic and sensitive individuals are prone to codependency in these situations. Depression is a serious illness, and many people with depression struggle to know where to begin in order to help themselves. The motivation is often lacking as a symptom of the illness. Consequently, the responsibility to motivate is often taken on by the loved ones, resulting in their own exhaustion and hindering their own plans. In a partnership, the codependent partner may refrain from making plans and enjoying life without their depressed loved one. They may experience feelings of guilt or hold onto the hope that one day they will be able to experience all the beauty in life together. This is where many people with commitment anxiety or a belief that life should not be enjoyable and easy for them become codependent. They end up in relationships with depressed individuals who reinforce this inner assumption, creating a slightly cloudy outlook on life.

Julia has been married to her depressed husband, Andreas, for twenty years. Since they met, Julia has fantasized about being able to bring joy into Andreas' life and be his saving anchor. She sees herself as a female support and soulmate for him. Unconsciously, Andreas' depression fulfills a challenge for Julia, proving to herself that she is capable of bringing light into darkness. This romantic notion originates from Julia's childhood. Her father was emotionally distant and introverted, and as a little girl, Julia would imagine that her presence and affection could brighten her father's face when she entered the room and climbed onto his lap. This imagination rarely came true, and her father's embrace never truly reached her heart. To this day, she continues her expedition from that time, struggling to be the savior for a lover she can free from their pain.

On the other hand, Andreas has fallen deep into depression due to the pain of his own childhood, which has robbed him of any joy in life. He explains to Julia, "It's as if I am disconnected from my heart. I am unable to experience genuine joy. If you want to be with me, you'll have to hold on a little longer until I resolve this."

However, due to the lack of motivation, Andreas finds it exceedingly difficult to confront his pain and seek therapy. Julia finds herself in a dilemma. On one hand, she wants to see her husband regain his radiance through her, as she is not yet aware of her own pattern. On the other hand, she wants Andreas to take personal responsibility. Thus, she repeatedly tries to persuade him to seek therapy or other forms of help to emphasize her support. This pattern solidifies over the years. Andreas remains stagnant because Julia carries him, and Julia becomes codependent. She unconsciously waits day in and day out for the miracle that will heal her husband, ideally through her love.

Who is Prone to Codependency?

Who is prone to codependency, and what does our human longing for belonging, bonding, and togetherness have to do with it? Codependence is an expression of an unsuccessful balance between autonomy and unity. We yearn for security and autonomy, for individuality and connection simultaneously. We need both aspects in order to develop in a healthy way and become independent, self-reliant members of a group or community who can adapt to the dynamics of the group while expressing our individuality.

Codependency testifies to the loss of one's own inner center, the active will for independence and self-efficacy, and the longing for fusion and conformity. The pendulum swings outside of oneself as the center of inner stability shifts outward to another person or the task found in connection. Consequently, many codependents stumble through life, feeling dizzy from the loss of their inner balance. They are torn between feeling lost and stable and the desire to sacrifice and care for the object of their dependency. However, since the person they focus on is also deeply unstable, the entire framework wobbles, pulling both parties further into depth and instability.

Empathy and compassion play important roles in codependency. Many codependents possess a high degree of empathy and the ability to deeply feel for others. They often forget about their own needs and live vicariously through the dependency of the other person. Behind this behavior hides a feeling of inferiority, which manifests itself in excessive admiration of others, as well as a desire for a sense of superiority that can be maintained through control.

Those who feel inferior often find themselves in codependent relationships with individuals they look up to. These relationships can involve narcissists, person with addiction, or highly manipulative people. Some codependents desperately seek a sense of home, a place where they can let go and feel safe. However, they do not find the inner stability that would allow them to seek a healthy environment. This would require them to be self-directed and engage on an equal footing with others. Instead, they find themselves in a state of lack, searching for a nurturing place without being nurturing themselves. Individuals who display a narcissistic posture, initially appearing as a reliable pillar of support, become objects of dependence for these codependents. However, they soon realize that the narcissist cannot provide what they truly long for: genuine attention, understanding, love, affection, and tenderness without selfish ulterior motives.

Dennis has never felt at home anywhere or with anyone. He has spent years traveling the world, considering himself a free-spirited traveler, a hippie. He boasts about his life as a homeless person, earning money through street art, but he never truly settles. Outwardly, he appears invulnerable, but inwardly, he feels ungrounded and alone. When he meets the tough and confident Bettina during his journey, he immediately falls in love with her. She seems to know what she wants, exudes confidence, and makes plans. However, Bettina is also struggling with addiction. Dennis quickly becomes entangled in her world and starts following her everywhere. He feels like he has found his social home. When Bettina experiences a drug-induced crash, Dennis is shocked to witness the transformation of his sassy, strong, show-off girlfriend. Suddenly, he feels more alone than ever before, as if his life is being pulled out from under him. It is only when Bettina recovers and returns to her lifestyle that Dennis regains the strength to pick himself up again. For many months, Bettina remains Dennis' social anchor. Whenever she feels good, she makes him feel safe and secure. Whenever she spirals downward, Dennis' sense of security is also threatened. What is striking about this connection is that Bettina tolerates Dennis in her presence only because he financially supports her. Much of Dennis' hard-earned money from street art flows into her hands, but she does not open her heart to him. She keeps him in line through small emotional gestures but remains self-focused and acts according to her own desires and dependencies. Dennis is driven further into codependency by his deep compassion towards her suffering. He gives money, time, and energy, receiving a sense of belonging in return.

Individuals who seek a sense of superiority often have a strong desire to support people with addiction, carry them, and be indispensable to them. They feel strong and confident when they are needed, and the person with addiction clings to them. This type of codependency can be difficult to identify, as the codependent slips into the role of the helpful Samaritan, displaying vigor, strength, and commitment. Deep down, however, they harbor a feeling of worthlessness when they are not needed. This particular attitude can perpetuate and even reinforce the person with addiction's dependency, as the codependent secretly does not want the other person to get well. Recovery could potentially lead to the codependent losing their sense of purpose and well-being.

Beatrice has four adult children, each struggling with different addiction patterns. One is addicted to cannabis, another to relationships, constantly changing partners after a few weeks. The third child is trapped in a toxic marriage, and the fourth child, at the age of twenty-five, still lives with her. Beatrice worries incessantly about all her children and keeps her home open to them. Each adult child has their own room, and Beatrice cooks for them whenever they visit.

Beatrice frequently shares her wish for her children to find a good path and be healthy with her friends. However, her codependent inner attitude compels her to excessively mother and overprotect her children, depriving them of the strength they need to stand on their own feet. Even as children, Beatrice took care of everything in their everyday lives. She made their breakfast sandwiches throughout their college years, patiently woke her eighteen-year-old son up multiple times every morning during his education, picked up all the children from parties in the middle of the night every weekend, and took on any costs and responsibilities for their youthful mistakes. She was considered the typical mother hen. This approach robbed her children of self-confidence in their own abilities, leaving them passive and helpless in various aspects of life.

Through her children's addictive patterns, Beatrice continues to feel superior, needed, and important, thus escaping the fear of loneliness and the feeling that she is not loved for who she truly is. She does not allow herself to shape her own life outside of her responsibilities towards her children. She is regularly admired and praised by friends and neighbors for her selfless dedication and motherly care over the years.

Underlying all codependent relationships is a sense of inferiority that places less importance on one's own needs than on those of others, particularly the suffering dependent caregiver. Empathetic and compassionate people who genuinely have good intentions and strive to do their best in relationships can easily fall into codependency. They identify themselves as kind, helpful, and caring and have grounded their behavior in these values. Discovering that these values can take on unhealthy traits is not an easy realization.

Our society heavily emphasizes social values such as helpfulness and support. Most individuals absorb these general values from an early age:

"Don't take toys away from weaker children!"

"Be considerate!"

"Comfort others when they are sad!"

"Be a good kid who helps others, and you'll have friends!"

"Make yourself useful, and I'll spend time with you!"

"Don't be selfish!"

Any action or attitude deemed selfish is considered negative and reprimanded during childhood without considering the child's developmental stage. Negative feelings must take a back seat, and young individuals must prove themselves to be social in order to receive recognition and positive feedback. Non-social behavior causes shame for parents in front of others and embarrassment for the child. Consequently, children learn that they must be gentle, kind, and nice in order to gain acceptance and be tolerated within their community. This belief often persists into adulthood, and individuals tend to view empathy and victimhood as consistently desirable traits. Unfortunately, many people experience exhaustion, fatigue, and even depression and burnout due to the one-sided focus on these social skills. They have never learned how to take care of themselves, and under the guise of morality, they assign greater importance to others and their suffering than to their own sphere of responsibility.

Empathy, compassion, and victimhood can serve as covers for both selfish goals (e.g., if I am kind, others won't reject me; if you need me, I will feel better) and one's own sense of inferiority (e.g., your suffering is greater than mine, I need to hold back, I am not worthy). Both aspects can strongly contribute to codependency. We continue engaging in certain behaviors only if the unhealed part of ourselves gains something from it and supports entrenched patterns, even if the exchange is unhealthy and detrimental to our well-being. The codependent individual avoids addressing internal issues by focusing outward and can suppress their own pain by busily caring for others. Codependency becomes an escape from one's own life. It affects not only individuals who have difficulty setting boundaries or lack resilience but also those who find it easier to shape other people's lives through their empathetic gifts rather than their own.

Maria is married to a depressed husband who has been suffering from his illness for years. He also numbs himself by spending hours surfing the Internet each day. Maria yearns to feel alive and free, but she doesn't allow herself to break free from her husband's melancholic energy. On one hand, she feels ashamed to experience joy when he is suffering. On the other hand, she feels responsible for supporting him and being there for him. She frequently experiences anger towards him and herself, wishing she could break free from the vicious cycle. However, whenever she indulges in daydreams of pursuing her own desires or even considering separation, her husband suddenly appears worse, as if he senses that Maria wants to distance herself and drain her energy from him. At that moment, Maria's empathy kicks in, and she returns to her familiar place, reassuring herself that she can prioritize her own needs once her husband is well.

Deep down, Maria hides another reason for her behavior: she has neglected self-care for so long that she doesn't truly know what else brings her joy or how she would genuinely like to live. She has become so consumed with sacrificing herself for her husband that she fears discovering a vast emptiness within herself and not knowing what to do with her life if she breaks free from codependency.

Therefore, her willingness to sacrifice is not solely driven by compassion and a sense of duty but also by the fear of being left alone to confront the unresolved issues and questions she has successfully avoided for years.

> **Inspiration**
>
> **Reflection Task: How to Recognize Codependent Situations**
>
> 1. Take a curious look at your social environment, if possible without judgment. Where can you identify areas that provide an ideal breeding ground for codependency?
>
> 2. Explore the realm of love songs and carefully analyze the lyrics: How can you detect expressions of codependency in different songs? Pay attention to intense emotions conveyed, such as helplessness, powerlessness, overwhelming passion, extreme devotion, fear of loss, and on-off relationships.
>
> You can also encounter codependent themes in novels, movies, and gripping stories: Often, the most compelling stories arise from codependent structures that take readers on an emotionally tumultuous journey. If all relationships were devoid of codependency and inner entanglements, there would hardly be any stories that evoke tears or elicit empathy.

Chapter 2
How Does Codependency Develop?

"Humans are inherently dependent; they are subject to death, aging, and illness (...). However, there is a distinction between recognizing one's own dependency and limitations, and fully surrendering to this dependency and idolizing the forces upon which one relies (...). The former reflects humility, while the latter represents self-degradation."

Erich Fromm

Background

Codependency can stem from various childhood scenarios, with the feeling of inferiority and the unsuccessful balance between adaptation and autonomy playing a crucial role. This balance is disrupted when the circumstances in childhood are unfavorable, lacking the necessary support for the child to freely and without constraint explore themselves and the world. A lack of physical, mental, and emotional security from primary caregivers or traumatic experiences contributes to this inhibiting climate.

The ideal scenario involves a child-friendly environment in which parents demonstrate the ability and willingness to prioritize their child's need for love, affection, and security over their own needs. They accompany the child through the years of natural and age-related dependence, allowing them to gradually discover their autonomy while feeling assured of their parents' affection and love, even when pursuing an independent path. This is achievable when parents have found a healthy balance between autonomy and connection, assuming their responsibility and viewing their time with their child as an investment that brings them joy. In this environment, the child feels valued, cherished, and a source of joy for their parents, fostering courage and a sense of confidence in exploring the world.

Every child desires cooperation with their parents and naturally tends to be loyal to their caregivers, as their actions, words, and worldview form the child's truth during their early years. A child with healthy and self-assured parents experiences the world as a secure and beautiful place where they can freely offer their existence as a gift. Conversely, a child with dependent and addicted parents, who reject, ignore, or devalue them, learns to perceive themselves as reflected by their parents:

- You are less important.
- You are not valuable.
- There is no place for you in this world.
- You are a burden.

The child also learns about the world based on the parents' behavior, reinforcing beliefs such as:

- The world is unsafe.
- Trust is elusive.
- Constant vigilance is necessary.
- One's true self and needs must be concealed.

Despite these circumstances, the child seeks connection through loyalty and cooperation. However, their self-expression is no longer freely flowing from within but is contingent upon an automatic scanning process:

- Is it safe to act this way?
- What is my parents' current mood?
- Should I be quiet?
- Should I be invisible?
- Should I help?

The child adapts to these circumstances in order to survive. The effects of a negative environment can be devastating, as the survival strategies developed during childhood persist into adulthood. As a result, codependents often choose relationships with dependent, incompetent, or addicted individuals who mirror the patterns of their parents. This environment feels familiar, as at least one parent was addicted, emotionally absent, abusive, depressed, narcissistic, or self-destructive. The codependent continues to internalize their self-perception:

- You are too much.
- You must conform.
- Your needs must remain unexpressed.

- Trust is forbidden.
- Emotions are to be suppressed.

The following survival strategies are developed during childhood characterized by dependency on caregivers:

- *Empathy:* The child learns to fully engage with their parents, offering understanding, compassion, and emotional support in order to mitigate potentially harmful situations. Unconsciously, they hope that their parents' frustration, rejection, or suffering will not be directed at them.

- *Willingness to help:* The child assumes important tasks and responsibilities that should be carried out by the parents, effectively taking on a parental role in many areas. This ensures that the child does not lose their parents to excessive demands, misfortune, or abandonment. Additionally, by being useful, the child avoids being completely ignored.

- *Suffering:* The child learns to emotionally suffer alongside their parents, demonstrating loyalty and internalizing the family's attitude towards life as a way to establish a sense of belonging.

- *Restraint:* The child suppresses the expression of their own needs to avoid overwhelming their parents. In some cases, this restraint may even be perceived as a service provided to the parents.

- *Rigidity:* The child represses and compartmentalizes unpleasant emotions such as anger, fear, powerlessness, and helplessness. Many codependents report that, for a long time, their childhood experiences did not seem bad or threatening. They have limited recollection of negative emotions. It is only through therapy, trauma work, and self-reflection that they begin to explore these repressed emotions.

As a child, Vanessa had an irascible, depressed father who was heavily addicted to alcohol. Her mother, on the other hand, sought solace in physical illness and adopted a dependent role. Being a housewife, she didn't earn any money and was plagued by existential fears due to the father's repetitive job losses caused by his depression and narcissistic personality structure.

As the older sibling of two children, Vanessa developed a strong sense of responsibility at an early age, taking on the role of emotional support for her mother and attempting to shield her brother from their father's violence. She recalls having the thought:

"If I can just be pretty, quiet, and inconspicuous, I can avoid my father's wrath."

While she adopted the survival strategy of self-sacrifice, helper, and empath, there was an internal struggle and a desperate cry for attention and freedom. The more she sacrificed herself for the sake of her family, the worse the situation seemed to become. When the pressure became unbearable, Vanessa sought solace in a secret life of friend-

ships and parties outside of her family structure during her youth. However, guilt weighed heavily on her, making it difficult for her to experience true joy. She suffered from the feeling of abandoning her family. Moreover, her father's constant threats of self-harm added to Vanessa's anxiety and panic. She blamed herself and feared that her hidden double life would push her father towards suicide.

As an adult, Vanessa realizes that her survival strategies have turned against her. She finds herself repeatedly entangled in codependent relationships where she assumes her old role. Her partners are consistently cold, dismissive, and often struggling with alcohol addiction. Vanessa attempts to convince her partners to quit drinking through flattery and special devotion. Despite yearning for freedom and desiring to end the relationship, she can't bring herself to leave her partners alone out of fear that they may harm themselves.

Hidden Goals

Alfred Adler's psychology offers an intriguing perspective on the secret goals that each person develops during their childhood experiences. These hidden goals are meant to help individuals overcome their feelings of inferiority and ultimately find a meaningful place in life and society. They aim to eliminate the sense of separation, isolation, and worthlessness. Unconsciously, these secret goals shape our actions, desires, dreams, and intermediate objectives, significantly influencing our relationships and our roles in connection with others. It goes far beyond a simple desire to be happy. At its core, the hidden goal revolves around what was lacking in one's childhood or where their deepest wounds lie concealed.

Some people strive to feel powerful, avoiding the fear of losing control by attempting to dominate others. Others, based on their experiences, harbor a deep fear of abandonment. Their secret goal is to avoid being alone at all costs, even if it means enduring significant pain. On the other hand, some individuals make it their secret goal to be irresistible or the only one. They go to great lengths to be as beautiful as possible, surpassing others in uniqueness, stunning appearance, and unquestioned acceptance. The list goes on and on.

"Once I'm rich, I will feel…"

"Once I'm an executive, I will feel…"

"Once I find my dream partner, I will feel…"

"Once I've convinced my partner to truly love me, I will feel…"

The answers to the secret goal lie not in the external achievements (beauty, wealth, etc.) but in the feeling of what we hope to attain. The feeling of finally arriving, being accepted, and recognized as valuable.

The more precisely we understand our secret goal, the more we can become aware of how it unconsciously shapes our decisions. Whom do we secretly aim to impress? Whom do we want to convince of our worth? Whom do we seek to convert, attract to our side, or pacify? Is it the image of our past mother or father? What role do we aspire to fulfill for someone? The number one, the indispensable, the one and only?

Understanding the secret goal can provide insight into why we find ourselves trapped in codependent entanglements and why we continue to repeat the same patterns. It can help us delve deeper into self-understanding, self-acceptance, and self-love. Up until this point, our secret goal has given us the strength to persevere, offering hope for healing our pain in the future.

However, as we become aware of the negative consequences associated with these secret goals, it is crucial to examine our strategies more closely. The goal itself is not the problem; the emotions we long for are valid. They are inherently human, seeking closeness, warmth, connection, freedom, and well-being. Yet, the old survival strategies we developed in childhood often no longer serve us today. This is where the codependent structures addressed in this book arise. They are the outcomes of our attachment to outdated self-protective patterns while pursuing our goals. Although we yearn for love with all our hearts, we struggle to allow this transformative love to thrive in healthy relationships.

Inspiration

Self-Reflection

Allocate sufficient time for this exercise to avoid feeling rushed, and find a place where you can feel comfortable and secure. Only engage in this exercise when you are emotionally stable.

Embark on an inner journey into your past. Observe the relevant scenes that surface and approach them with curiosity, using the following questions:

"What seemingly insatiable longing has emerged in this moment?"
"What pain was triggered during that moment?"
"As a result, what inner goal have I unconsciously chosen for my future to resolve this internal conflict?"
"How does this inner goal manifest in my life and relationships through codependent behavior?"

Emotionally open yourself to this exercise if you are able to, but be aware that memories and feelings may arise that require your attention and time.

Write down your answers to these questions, as doing so will facilitate a deeper understanding and allow your insights to firmly establish themselves in your consciousness.

Needs Behind Codependency

Codependency is not a recognized diagnostic term in the clinical field. However, it sheds light on the mental suffering that arises from deep-seated needs. These needs are shared by all individuals, but codependents lack the ability to respond to them in a responsible and self-loving manner.

The underlying needs behind codependency can be identified as follows:

Value for Others
Codependents have a deep desire to convince the dependent or loved one to change their behavior through acts of self-sacrifice. At its core, this longing is rooted in the fundamental need for a sense of worthiness. They yearn to be seen as valuable enough by the dependent, hoping that this recognition will prompt the dependent to release their addiction, thus avoiding any harm or loss to the codependent. Behind this yearning lies the inner child who craves to be the top priority of their parent, seeking love, care, and wholehearted acceptance. The codependent believes that the dependent individual's ability to overcome their own challenges is a testament to their love and dedication to the codependent.

Tasha continuously seeks out partners who struggle with addiction and dependence in various ways. She immerses herself in daydreams, envisioning a prince on a white horse who triumphs over obstacles to conquer her heart. She yearns for her partners to harness their inner strength, confront their own demons, and emerge as liberated individuals capable of carrying her on their shoulders. Tasha expresses her belief that men who shy away from facing their personal challenges are uninteresting and unworthy of her. Reflecting on her childhood, she recalls her parents, who themselves battled addiction, frequently gossiping about the so-called "upper class" who seemed to effortlessly glide through life without facing hardships. They jokingly remarked about their privileged lives where everything seemed to fall into their laps without any effort. Tasha witnessed her parents tirelessly struggling to provide for their four children while seeking solace in intoxication and addiction. This experience left her torn, powerless, and helpless. The only option that seemed viable to her was to embrace a fairy-tale notion of her own identity and possess a magical power to inspire others. Consequently, even to this day, Tasha is driven by the desire to transform her partners through her very existence, helping them conquer any obstacles that stand in their way.

Control

Codependents often attempt to exert control over their own life situation by trying to control the person with addiction issues. This can manifest in behaviors such as monitoring their drug and alcohol consumption by drinking alongside them or picking them up from the pub late at night. The underlying motivation behind this control is the fear of becoming entangled and dependent on the person with addiction issues, as well as the fear of experiencing economic, emotional, or social ruin. The desire for control stems from the need for security and a sense of connection within a social network.

Codependency in Relationships

Matthias and his wife have been a couple for three years. Matthias met Iris at a party and didn't view her inclination for intoxicants as an issue. Quite the opposite, Iris introduced Matthias, who was naturally reserved, to exhilarating realms filled with music, dancing, and late-night adventures. She injected vitality into his previously mundane student life. However, after getting married and moving in together, Matthias adopted a more settled domestic lifestyle. He has been working diligently and providing financial support to Iris, who continues to allocate a significant portion of his modest earnings towards alcohol and parties. As friends and relatives increasingly pose critical questions and express concern about Matthias, a fear grows within him that Iris may not mature in the future. He begins to perceive her behavior from a different perspective. The initial admiration gives way to apprehension regarding his reputation and the strain it places on his work life, as he spends countless sleepless nights waiting for her return.

Matthias attempts to communicate with Iris, but her response is one of anger, insinuating that he is attempting to control her. "You simply can't tolerate being such a bore! I refuse to be confined," she screams before leaving their shared apartment for two nights. Matthias becomes increasingly burdened, worrying about Iris and shouldering the blame for her departure without realizing that she manipulates him through her outbursts of anger. He becomes entangled in a whirlpool of concern, desperately trying to mitigate the negative consequences stemming from Iris' lifestyle choices.

Freedom and Liveliness

Some codependents gravitate towards individuals who already embody the role of outsiders and rebels. In doing so, they unconsciously hope to escape from social pressures and obligations, only to realize too late that by aligning themselves with these individuals, they are entering into a renewed state of dependency. The outcome often includes social isolation and despair, which further drives them deeper into codependency. They find themselves caught between two worlds: not feeling at home in their familiar environment and failing to find true freedom, even in rebellion and association with an unstable individual. The yearning for freedom and autonomy is particularly intense in this scenario. The codependent lives a life riddled with contradictions and a sense of confinement, while the desire for vibrancy and freedom within them remains fervent. It becomes challenging for them to attain this freedom through self-empowerment and relying on their own inner strength.

Florence is a single parent living in bustling Brooklyn with her daughter. She feels overwhelmed by the obligations of her everyday life and yearns for a change. She comes across Arnold, an attractive individual she meets online, who entices her with promises of embarking on a journey to emigrate and explore the world together. After months of flirting and two meetings, Florence cannot resist the allure: she decides to move with her daughter to Arnold's place in the countryside. Their plan is to embark on a trip around the world from there, and Florence envisions a romantic adventure where she will experience newfound freedom and her daughter will have a father figure.

However, reality unfolds differently. The starting time of their journey keeps getting postponed, and Florence gradually realizes that Arnold is completely unreliable and lacks commitment and responsibility. The romantic ideals burst when Florence discovers that Arnold frequently indulges in marijuana and lives a marginalized life on the outskirts of the idyllic village, which initially seemed to be their shared social setting. Florence is now faced with the harsh truth that she made a wrong decision, putting herself and her daughter in a difficult situation. She attempts to wake Arnold up and persuade him to hold onto their shared dream, but Arnold becomes increasingly detached and reveals his true nature. He makes grand promises but fails to deliver the freedom Florence longs for.

Years later, Florence reflects on this phase of her life and acknowledges, "I yearned so deeply for freedom that I was lured by this untamed bird without considering the price. I found myself entangled in feelings of guilt towards my daughter, as well as a sense of inadequacy in taking responsibility. I allowed myself to be blinded, and to make matters worse, I realized that Arnold was a reflection of my own inability to take responsibility. It was only after months of inner struggle that I made the decision to let go and free myself from the codependent structure, finding my way back to our previous life with my daughter. I made sure to grant myself more freedom and pursued a new job that brings me joy. In doing so, I reclaimed the freedom I had projected onto Arnold."

Innocence

The need for innocence resides deep within us, as we desire to be included and not excluded from the bigger picture. In our society, a culture that embraces mistakes is slowly emerging, but many individuals still struggle to attain a sense of innocence by externalizing blame rather than embracing a holistic and loving perspective that transcends notions of guilt and innocence, good and evil.

Children often say, "I didn't do anything," out of fear of punishment or withdrawal of love. As adults, those who yearn for innocence have often learned in the past that the shadow side of a person is inherently bad and deserving of judgment. Especially in families with strong moral codes, children tend to blame each other when accidents happen or something is broken. Even when parents resort to violence, it becomes crucial for a child to disown any blame in order to feel safe.

As adults, individuals from such families may continue the pattern of never admitting fault. However, mishaps still occur, and our own shadows exist. If we haven't learned to embrace our imperfections and love ourselves unconditionally, we tend to project our disliked qualities onto others. This projection necessitates the presence of a scapegoat, someone who openly acknowledges and embodies their own shadow sides and secret inclinations. This dynamic can be observed in social groups, as well as in love or familial relationships. A relative, partner, or member of a clique is chosen as the scapegoat and is thereafter held responsible for everything that goes wrong. Codependency arises when the codependent, usually unconsciously, contributes to the perpetuation of this disempowering situation while being dependent on the identified scapegoat. The codependent supports the dependent or troubled individual where possible but simultaneously places all blame on them:

"I'm late because I was checking up on Andreas."

"I couldn't complete my project properly because this situation is causing me tremendous stress."

"I missed the appointment because Andreas had another episode."

"Andreas prevented me from doing that."

"I can't change my life because Andreas is always there."

Inspiration

Do you have an idea of how codependency might be manifesting in your own life? Is there someone in your life who holds immense importance to you, but whose life situation simultaneously drains your energy and causes you great worry?

What are your secret hopes and longings for this person? What change would bring you infinite happiness, even though you find it difficult to believe in it? What inner image of this person, filled with wholeness, encourages you to strengthen your support and not lose hope?

Take the time to describe in great detail what your ideal relationship with this person would look like if they were in a healthy state. Allow yourself to engage in intense daydreams and let your longing imagination take over.

Then, in equal detail, describe the reality of the current situation. What emotions do you struggle with in relation to this person and the relationship? What repetitive thoughts occupy your mind? What kind of suffering do you endure within this relationship? What unrealistic demands do you place on them?

Consider the following prompts to aid in your self-reflection:
- I deeply wish that the person I feel codependent on would...
- To be honest, I attempt to exert control over what... does because...
- It would be easier for me to detach if...
- I am afraid to let go because I fear that...
- I believe I could bring about the following change in the person by...
- This person means so much to me because...
- I believe I mean to this person...

Self-Love Reflection

As you continue your journey of discovering more about codependency, it can be beneficial to cultivate a habit of consciously doing something for yourself once a week, or even every day, that brings you joy and nurtures your well-being:

- Enjoy a peaceful cup of coffee without any interruptions.
- Finally start reading that book you've been interested in for a long time.
- Listen to music mindfully and with full presence.
- Engage in a spiritual practice or meditation that resonates with you.
- Express and communicate your needs effectively.
- ...

By engaging in these small acts of self-love, you create an atmosphere of appreciation and care for yourself. Remember, it's not just about what you do, but how you do it. Even a mindful, loving breath can bring comfort and upliftment to your being.

Chapter 3
Living in Codependence

"Do you want to become dependent on people whom you despise?"

Jean-Jacques Rousseau

Contempt

The opening quote from Jean-Jacques Rousseau is intentionally chosen to be exaggerated in this chapter: "Do you want to become dependent on people whom you despise?" Codependency does not always involve obvious contempt. However, contempt does not start when we spit at someone's feet or call them names. It begins in small ways, such as when we try to change or control other people. Contempt means lacking respect. Codependency is a process of lacking respect, both for ourselves and for the person whose behavior we are enduring. We blame them for our suffering because we can't let go, feel trapped, and experience a loss of self-esteem. We seek a sense of self-worth by sacrificing ourselves. Dependence that arises from unhealthy patterns is, in itself, an act of contempt.

Healthy dependency occurs when a person is fundamentally cared for by another who willingly takes on that responsibility. This is especially true in parent-child relationships.

As we grow into adulthood, we are meant to outgrow this natural dependency and cultivate our own inner growth. ***Codependency, however, is remaining in a dependent relationship with someone who cannot provide the care we need.*** We sense this incapacity in the other person, but due to our conditioning, we keep seeking reasons to stay connected. This can lead to anger directed at ourselves and the other person, feeling trapped, and the inability to grow and develop. One of the most important resources we need for healthy development is lacking: ***respect for our own dignity and acting with integrity.***

Taking responsibility for our own dignity is not an easy task. If we were not taught about our dignity when it was appropriate, as adults, we often have to go through a painful process of discovering it for ourselves. Every new or recurring conflict offers an opportunity to become aware of our dignity in the given situation and to act accordingly. However, this is easier said than done because our inner child longs for a parent figure, preferably similar to our own, to guide us. But this plan is doomed to fail because the person we choose does not possess the resources to fulfill this role. Moreover, even a part of the codependent within ourselves rebels against this dynamic because the part that desires autonomy knows, "This is not right. I am no longer a child."

If we continue to hold onto the childlike desire for others to show us our own dignity before we do so ourselves, we hinder our growth toward healthy autonomy. This resistance to self-efficacy generates anger, and that anger gives rise to contempt. Since it is less painful to externalize contempt than to direct it inward, we use the other person in the codependent relationship as a target, reinforcing the codependent dynamic.

The consequence of such a dynamic can manifest in codependent behavior, oscillating between **rebellion** and **submission** to the caregiver. The codependent desires a relationship of equality and freedom but seeks it with someone who cannot provide such dynamics. This leads to control, manipulation, and disputes arising from trivial matters. Below are typical examples from everyday life:

- A mother in a codependent relationship with her depressed partner finds herself caught in a cycle of intense love (submission) and anger (rebellion) toward him. Understanding that he is unwell, she empathetically attaches herself to him by trying to support him even more. However, she periodically becomes angry at him for not taking responsibility for their shared child and leaving her alone with numerous daily tasks. During these moments, she desires to shake her partner awake or separate from him immediately.

- A man in love with a highly irritable woman vacillates between anger (rebellion) and submission due to his secret fear of her and his feelings of powerlessness. Simultaneously, he relies on her due to his own strong sense of inner weakness. He attempts to control her choleric outbursts by kindly de-escalating the situation and disregarding his own needs. When he is angry, he directs his anger inward, berating himself in her presence ("I'm so stupid!").

- A woman who has given up her job to support her narcissistic husband's career vacillates between anger and submission. She hopes to win her husband's heart through her sacrifice but simultaneously feels contempt for herself for not safeguarding her own dignity. While her sacrifice is meant to be manipulative, it fails to evoke any emotion in her husband. Consequently, she creates her own emotional escape by engaging in a clandestine affair, which provides her with a sense of control.

- A woman who has chosen a highly sensitive and empathetic but extremely passive husband vacillates between anger and submission. She desires an active partner while also feeling obligated to be grateful that her husband is not an irritable screamer as her father was. She experiences anger due to being emotionally stagnant: she hopes each day that her husband will show more initiative in their relationship, yet she submits by trying to convince him to be proactive through excessive accommodation.

- A man who has finally retired after devoting his life and finances to his alcoholic wife vacillates between anger and submission. He is uncertain about how to spend his time without her while simultaneously longing for the freedom from her demanding ways. He expresses anger towards his wife yet continues to do everything for her.

- A woman married to a manic husband vacillates between rebellion and submission, depending on her husband's current phase. When he is depressed, she submits and makes herself small, speaking softly to avoid appearing superior and provoking him. Secretly, she fears his endless anger lurking behind his depression. When he is exuberant, she becomes angry because she feels powerless as he makes impulsive and irresponsible decisions that negatively impact her. She threatens separation but remains in the relationship as her threats fail to instigate any change in her husband's behavior.

Confusion

In addition to the feeling of contempt, codependency is often marked by a sense of confusion. Emotional, mental, and sometimes even physically palpable confusion arises from the dynamics of the shifted center, where the codependent's own center has shifted outward, becoming dependent on their partner or relative as a point of reference. As a result, codependent individuals don't feel secure in their own truth and opinions, and they are unable to freely and openly express them to their relatives. On the other hand, the relative may also be deeply confused due to their own dependency or hold rigid attitudes that leave no room for contradiction. The codependent relationship acts like an emotional corset, providing support to the codependent but not aligning with their authentic self, causing them to lose sight of their own identity when connected to the relative.

The feeling of confusion may not necessarily permeate all of the codependent's relationships and areas of life. Many codependents report feeling confused only when they are around or connected to the codependent relative. Outside of these relationships, they may be self-reliant, independent, and successful in various aspects of their lives. They maintain healthy relationships, pursue fulfilling careers, and are good parents as long as the relative or partner is not present.

However, this confusion can passively affect other areas of their lives. Depending on how much space the codependent relationship takes up, other aspects may suffer from lost time and energy. Many codependents could reach their full potential if the unhealthy relationship did not hinder their progress. Confusion about one's identity, ability to make good choices, and live independently also becomes apparent during self-reflection. When codependents begin to recognize their patterns and become aware of what is happening, they often feel deep fear: How can I tend to have such unhealthy attitudes? What is wrong with me? Can I even trust my own perception and judgment?

Confusion can be intensified by heightened sensitivity and empathy. Codependents become deeply entangled in the lives and experiences of others, blending their own feelings with those of the other person. They view their own decisions through the lens of the other person's opinion or excessively consider the condition and needs of their reference partner in their decision-making process. In other words, they don't allow their own energy to flow freely and naturally.

As children, codependents often develop a radar for the needs and emotions of those around them. They needed to possess a heightened sensitivity and empathetic ability to discern the underlying dynamics with their parents or caregivers, adapting and cooperating to create a sense of safety. The childhood environment of a person prone to codependency was often characterized by inauthentic communication, subtle aggression, withdrawal of love, and hidden negative feelings. As a result, the child relied on their radar to detect what their parent was not openly expressing. Some individuals recall their parents' sudden mood changes, shifting from seemingly good moods to anger or overwhelm, which were not readily apparent without this radar. This constant unpredictability created an environment that felt like a ticking time bomb, ready to explode at any moment.

These empathetic abilities are carried into adulthood, where codependents use them in their dependence on their partner or relative to decipher their inauthentic and unreliable communication and behavior, seeking a sense of security. However, this leads to further confusion. The codependent finds it challenging to address conflicts openly, even when sensing that something is wrong. They are aware that the dependent person is unable or unwilling to show themselves genuinely and engage in truthful communication. Conversations often devolve into manipulative mud-slinging, veering away from the actual topic, and both parties lose themselves in irrelevant distractions, hurling accusations at each other. In some cases, the confusion becomes so overwhelming that both parties struggle to recall the original reason for their dispute. This confusion becomes an ordeal for the codependent. While they understand what is happening, the other person does not create the space for open communication. If the codependent tries to express themselves clearly, they face defensive strategies such as stonewalling, aggressiveness, escape, blackmail attempts, and other manipulative behaviors.

Typical everyday examples:

- A codependent woman experiences confusion as soon as her narcissistic partner enters the room. Just moments before, she had clear plans for the day, but now she sees everything from her partner's perspective and anticipates his criticism even before he voices it. She feels confused, oppressed, and trapped. This confusion robs her of joy in her own plans, causing her to change them without even discussing them with her partner. She ends up planning something that she assumes he will like, often sacrificing her own desires in the process.

- Another codependent woman feels confused about her dreams and aspirations for the future. She takes care of her alcoholic father, who financially supports her in order to pursue her own plans. However, he constantly belittles her and undermines her confidence, labeling her as incompetent. Due to her caregiving responsibilities, she was unable to complete vocational training. This leaves her confused about her own ability to achieve her dreams independently, without her father's support.

- A codependent man finds himself constantly questioning, "What is the right thing to do?" He is in a codependent relationship with his dissatisfied and unhappy boss, who exercises control over the entire team. Despite holding a high position in the company, which he owes to his choleric boss, he lives in fear of angering him and losing his job. He desires to start his own business but feels confused about whether he can trust himself to break away from his current job and stand on his own economically. He also worries about the repercussions of leaving his boss alone and potentially contributing to the company's downfall.

- Another codependent woman grapples with confusion regarding her identity as an adult woman versus her internalized feeling of being a little girl. Her partner is highly controlling and domineering, often speaking to her as if she were a child. However, he also admires her womanly charm and meets her as an adult in certain moments. The man's addiction to keeping her subdued stems from his fear of strong women. The woman, in turn, fears her own strength and self-efficacy, projecting this fear onto her partner. This creates significant confusion about her sense of identity, leading her to seek guidance from her partner.

- A codependent woman witnesses her alcoholic partner going through the grieving process after the recent loss of his mother. He frequently cries and openly shares his grief, but the woman struggles to sense the authenticity of his sorrow since he is constantly inebriated. His grief appears superficial, almost like a performance. Subconsciously, the codependent woman responds with less empathy and emotional warmth due to the partner's inner numbness, unintentionally mirroring his true emotional state. In response, the partner becomes angry and accuses her of being emotionally distant, failing to confront his own inner detachment. This creates a profound sense of confusion for the codependent woman as she finds herself publicly criticized for her empathetic expression, a quality she does not wish to deny. She experiences guilt as a result.

Denial

Denial is another significant phenomenon in codependency. It works hand in hand with contempt and involves minimizing, suppressing, and disregarding one's own self and needs. Denial plays a crucial role in the development of codependency, as it allows for the outsourcing of needs, a shift of one's center outward, and the denial of inner truth. Confusion often accompanies this process, as ignoring the inner truth becomes necessary to maintain the codependent situation. Denial is closely intertwined with the self-preservation instinct, which ensures a delicate balance. These two forces work together to prevent the codependent from completely losing themselves in the unhealthy relationship. Just when the codependent's inner truth begins to resurface and take over, momentarily breaking free from codependency's grasp, it is swiftly submerged once again into the swamp of denial. If the inner truth were to remain on the surface and the codependent was to stop ignoring it, the codependent relationship would be jeopardized. This triggers fears of separation, independence, the responsibilities that come with realization, and the inevitable pain that accompanies the process of dissolving dependency and reclaiming one's own center.

Denial serves as a defense mechanism to maintain the status quo and perpetuate codependency. By subsuming themselves and their needs to the other person, codependents avoid confronting the unpleasant feelings that would arise from outgrowing the connection.

Here are some typical examples of denial:

- A woman in a codependent relationship with her sick sister denies her desire to emigrate abroad because she does not want to abandon her sister. In doing so, she evades the fear of the unknown, suppressing her inner truth that overcoming fear through courage is possible.

- A mother who is codependent on her drug-addicted son denies her inner truth to seek new fulfilling partnerships, diverting herself from the task of caring for her son. This allows her to escape her fear of rejection by men on an equal footing.

- A man denies his inclination for adventure and finds himself in codependency with his wife, who suffers from an anxiety disorder. He suppresses his inner truth that life is meant to be felt and experienced, and instead hides behind a seemingly selfless attitude towards his wife, refraining from causing her fear. In this way, he avoids confronting his own fear of life's immense power.

- A woman denies her inner truth, which forbids her to be dishonest. Her husband cheats on their tax returns, and if she were to uphold her truth, it would put the relationship at risk. So, she ignores her guilty conscience and trivializes her husband's behavior. In self-preservation, she convinces herself that she is not guilty and has no involvement. Nevertheless, she remains connected to the energy of her husband's deceit through the relationship and suffers as a result.

- A woman denies her deep desire for a romantic relationship in which her partner independently strives to know her heart on a deeper level. Instead, she seeks a partner who is incapable of such intrinsic motivation due to her dependency. This allows her to escape the fear that a capable partner might not take this step out of inability but rather out of disinterest. The pain associated with this realization would be too overwhelming for her. By becoming codependent, she secures a partner who stays with her, even if it doesn't align with her deepest desire.

In addition to contempt, confusion, and denial, hope, faith, and altruism also shape the everyday experience of a codependent individual. These positive aspects work as counterbalancing forces, aiming to maintain a positive outlook on the codependent relationship and avoid separation and the accompanying pain. The interplay of these conflicting dynamics creates a constant back-and-forth in the lives of codependents. They oscillate between themselves and the other person, between dependency and the pursuit of freedom, between despair and happiness, and between the quest for inner peace and the deep understanding that it can only be attained by letting go and dissolving codependency. However, guilt and fear often stand in their way, acting as barriers that prevent them from pulling the ripcord and breaking free.

Hope

Hope often emerges when there is a glimpse of changed behavior from the dependent individual. The codependent clings to the promise of improvement, with the individual suddenly becoming attentive, insightful, and seeking help for a short period. Hope also arises when the codependent has a good day and feels a sense of empowerment:

- I can still save him/her.
- I don't have to endure much longer.
- Miracles can happen!
- The power of love can conquer all.

However, this hope is deceptive because it rests on the unstable foundation of the dependent individual's fluctuating behavior and the codependent's excessive self-sacrifice. Both foundations are bound to fail in the long run. The dependent's behavior is not conscious or reliable, lacking personal responsibility, values, or a strong inner character orientation that the codependent can rely on. Similarly, the codependent's willingness to sacrifice will eventually reach its limits, either due to external factors such as burnout, illness, or a stroke of fate or through inner boundaries that the codependent finally recognizes and takes seriously.

But in the initial moment, the feeling of hope provides strength and the illusion that the fog is lifting. The codependent wants to exhaust every possibility and truly believe that they have given them all before considering giving up. Hope helps them persevere and continue the game. It acts like a drug, instilling positive images of the future and creating a belief that their attitude can positively influence and control what unfolds.

Here are some typical examples:

- A codependent man repeatedly forgives his wife, who cheats and tearfully apologizes time and time again.

- A codependent woman struggles to see her aggressive husband as bad and establish boundaries. She holds onto the belief that one day he will recognize his inherent goodness and stop yelling at her. When he apologizes and remains friendly for a few days, she believes that change is possible.

- A codependent woman has been waiting for thirty years for a romantic relationship with her narcissistic husband. Even after they start living in separate apartments because he moved out, she still clings to hope for change.

The codependent form of hope mimics genuine hope that individuals need to break free from unhealthy patterns together or on their own and to heal. Hope is essential for the healing process, as it provides the conviction that starting anew is possible and serves as a driving force to take necessary steps. We can also refer to this beneficial type of hope as faith. True faith involves inner guidance, focusing on our inner resources and positive possibilities. It is not a mere coincidence but a conscious choice. This choice empowers us, reminds us of our self-efficacy, and unlike the helpless hope in codependency, becomes a powerful tool towards freedom.

Good Faith
Good faith arises when individuals struggle to confront the pain of their inner child and the resulting shadow aspects. They fear being overwhelmed by their own shadows and tend to ignore them. At its core, good faith toward others is a way of avoiding one's own inner shadow parts. Those who exhibit good faith often struggle to admit their mistakes, deflect blame, emphasize inner purity, and take confrontations personally.

Good faith is not only directed toward others but also involves turning a blind eye to one's own unhealed and negatively impacting aspects. Gullible codependents are often found in relationships where the other person is seen as the "black sheep" while they position themselves as innocent victims. They believe that the other person has destroyed their life, yet they cannot bring themselves to break free and let go. They remain in the codependent relationship to perpetuate this pattern. In doing so, they avoid taking responsibility for their part in the harmful dynamic. They see the other person as the "black sheep" but fail to recognize their own borderline shadow field.

Bona fide codependents are characterized by their failure to take responsibility for their role in the jointly created dynamic.

Here are some typical examples:

- A codependent mother repeatedly believes her son's adventurous stories about finding money, even though he claims it is missing from her purse. She avoids the responsibility she bears as a mother for her son's development and refuses to acknowledge any mistakes she may have made in his upbringing.

- The codependent woman who has been eagerly waiting for her husband to change for thirty years is unaware of any guilt, despite subjecting him to daily criticism. She believes he deserves the criticism, and she feels powerless under her husband's coldness. She shies away from the responsibility she shares with her husband for the state of their relationship. Her inner battle cry is: "Guilt must be far away from me! Since I am suffering, the blame must solely lie with the other person."

- ♦ A bona fide man repeatedly signs dubious employment contracts because he cannot fathom that others could be deceitful enough to cheat him. He secretly fears his own potential to prioritize his self-interest and resort to fraudulent means if necessary and thus ignores this aspect in others. Additionally, he avoids taking responsibility for his own well-being, as he has never learned to assert himself. Consequently, he finds himself trapped in one predicament after another, unable to see the recurring pattern.

Good faith, like hope, can have a healing effect on relationships of any kind when approached with full awareness and personal responsibility. In such cases, it takes on a different name and arises from a different source: trust. Trust stems from a foundation of healthy primal trust, where an individual knows that the world is not inherently hostile and that they are welcome and can find their place in the environment—they belong. A person who lives with trust can confront the painful and negative effects of their own wounds and those of others without feeling existentially threatened by them. Good faith, on the other hand, is an attempt to create an ideal world through ignorance, one that excludes the unpleasant parts.

Altruism

Altruism is a highly revered and often idealized human virtue that involves selfless and unselfish behavior, considering and serving others. At first glance, this attitude may seem commendable, but in the context of codependency, altruism can become a trap. Many codependents justify their sacrificial behavior with an altruistic mindset, attempting to portray the codependent situation in a positive light. They don't want to admit that their behavior does not arise from freedom and that their willingness to sacrifice is not truly altruistic. In fact, the codependent part can benefit from this dynamic, albeit in an unhealthy manner. The inability to let go of the other person and take personal responsibility is transfigured and presented as a loving willingness to serve and support the other.

Here are some typical examples:

- A codependent woman refuses to leave her alcoholic partner and continues to provide him with money, shelter, and attention, despite his repeated aggressive behavior towards her. She justifies her actions by claiming that she selflessly wants to help the man get a second chance in life.

- A codependent man overextends himself in his commitment to his company, going beyond his actual capacity, and convinces himself that his dedication greatly benefits the company. Unbeknownst to him, he benefits in a hidden way by being able to perceive himself as part of something bigger and by avoiding feelings of loneliness and insignificance.

- A codependent woman invests all her money in the education and extravagant lifestyle of her twenty-year-old son, who becomes increasingly demanding and unconstructive. She explains her self-sacrifice as an act of selflessness, while in reality, she is escaping her constant feeling of guilt for not having done enough for her son in earlier years.

Altruism is initially a neutral attitude that can develop on either healthy or wounded ground, leading to healing or destruction. However, when altruism is used to rationalize codependency, it solidifies the unhealthy pattern and supports dependency, addiction, and toxic entanglement.

The healthy counterpart to altruism is genuine devotion, which arises from a mindset of holistic self-love and healthy boundaries. True giving of oneself can only be sustained when it is a conscious choice made in freedom, accompanied by the ability to say no, and aligned with one's own values and inner truth. True surrender requires a clear stance. We give when our inner selves are strengthened, and we have taken good care of ourselves. We do not give beyond our means. We decide to whom and where we direct our giving. We offer ourselves when it fulfills us and doesn't deplete us. Genuine devotion doesn't necessarily involve suffering. Many people mistakenly believe that altruism is inevitably linked to suffering and confuse the suffering that arises from dependency and unhealthy attachments with the authentic pain that can emerge when people make themselves vulnerable and open their hearts. When pain arises from a healthy, loving attitude, it can be a sign of genuine surrender. Suffering from dependency feels constricting and foggy; it drains energy and enables entanglement.

Experience

In this chapter, we delve into the lives of three individuals who suffer from codependency and observe how their daily lives are shaped by this condition. Through their stories, we witness both the internal and external pain and consequences that most codependent people experience.

Example 1: Marlene's codependency on her mother's drug addiction.

It all began with a prescription for a strong painkiller to alleviate Marlene's mother's back pain, which developed after her pregnancy. From a young age, Marlene perceived her mother as physically and emotionally weak, plagued by poor health. Her mother attributed her suffering to the challenging circumstances of being a single parent and the abandonment by her ex-partner. She openly shared her mental unhappiness with Marlene. As a result, Marlene grew up with the belief that she needed to be a loving and uncomplicated daughter to her mother in order to alleviate her mother's suffering. She was deeply affected by her mother's constant comparisons to Marlene's father: "You look like your father." "That's what your father would have said." "Make sure you don't turn out like your father!" Marlene yearned to please her mother and contribute to her relief. Consequently, she never mentioned missing her father and held onto the hope of one day meeting him. Marlene also limited her social activities with friends, as her main role was to massage her mother after her work shifts, offer encouragement, and instill hope. However, her mother's physical pain grew increasingly severe, leading to her losing her job and becoming dependent on painkillers.

Marlene vividly recalls an incident where her mother collapsed on the bathroom floor due to an overdose of sleeping pills and remained there overnight until Marlene found her the next morning. From that point on, the pills dictated their everyday lives. Marlene became consumed with fear of a similar event recurring, and she attempted to influence and control her mother's medication intake through gentle coaxing and seemingly casual inquiries.

Even in her teenage years, Marlene remained closely connected to her mother. When she eventually moved out, she chose an apartment across the street to provide ongoing support. As her mother lived on welfare and complained about not having enough money to afford the increasingly expensive painkillers, Marlene continuously offered financial assistance from her modest income as an educator.

As time went on, Marlene developed a growing desire to focus on her own life, attend to her own concerns, and honor her own needs. However, engaging in conversations with her mother made this nearly impossible, as any mention of her own experiences would be overshadowed by her mother's self-centered attention-seeking behavior. One day, Marlene reached her breaking point. She made the decision to ask her mother about her father and embark on a search to find him. In response, her mother broke down in tears, accusing Marlene of wanting to betray her and side with her father, claiming that he had ruined her entire life. Clutching her back in pain, her mother shook her head in tears and left the room.

Question 1: How can codependency be identified in Marlene's behavior?

- Marlene is always cautious not to criticize her mother.
- She seeks to control their interactions through subtle hints and coaxing.
- She strives to be a dutiful daughter.
- She makes all life decisions contingent on her mother's well-being and her role in her mother's life.
- She neglects her own needs.
- She maintains physical proximity to her mother at all times.
- She avoids, as long as possible, discussing topics that may lead to conflict.

Question 2: What internal motivation/trap might cause Marlene to remain in codependency?

Marlene's codependency on her mother's drug addiction is fueled by the entangled nature of their relationship. The roles of parent and child have become reversed, with Marlene carrying the weight of her mother's life and keeping her afloat. This pattern of behavior is thus supported and reinforced. The mother's victim mentality has a significant impact on their bond, leading Marlene to feel ashamed of her desire to connect with her father and associating feelings of guilt towards her mother with this longing. Marlene serves as both an anchor and a mirror for her mother's unforgiveness towards her father. This emotional irresponsibility on her mother's part keeps Marlene trapped in a connection filled with guilt and shame. Additionally, Marlene receives minimal attention from her mother, which she only receives when she goes above and beyond to help and support her. These small moments of praise and gratitude serve as encouragement for Marlene to continue in the hope that one day everything will be well again and she can rely on her mother. Typical statements from her mother include:

"If I didn't have you."

"I'm so glad you exist."

"I've always done my best for you."

"Don't leave me alone, you make me so happy. You are so good."

"It's good that we're sticking together."

Question 3: How does Marlene's own physical and emotional sensation manifest?

As a young adult, Marlene frequently experiences a sense of being physically constricted. When she feels anger, her legs become restless, but she is afraid to fully embrace and express her anger. She fears that if she were to fully feel this intense anger, she would lose control and cause harm. Dry skin and the urge to scratch herself all over further contribute to the feeling of being trapped in her own body. When in the presence of her mother, Marlene instinctively lowered her head and raised her shoulders. When her mother pours out her tales of suffering onto Marlene, she feels a lump in her throat and occasionally an impulse to push her mother against a wall or physically attack her. At night, Marlene sometimes dreams of pushing her mother down a slope, which fills her with deep shame. The next day, she tries even harder to be kind to her mother, which only intensifies the internal pressure and brings forth more anger. Marlene is caught in a cycle of guilt, shame, and inner rebellion. However, since her inner rebellion finds limited expression, she attempts to communicate her feelings through bodily sensations and dreams.

Question 4: How does the codependent relationship affect other areas of Marlene's life?

Due to the restraint she has learned within the codependent dynamic, Marlene behaves like a subdued presence in her interactions with peers and colleagues. She often feels as if her voice is stifled, unable to find words when she wants to express herself. Those around her have grown accustomed to Marlene taking on any task or request without resistance. However, some perceptive colleagues notice that she is becoming increasingly careless and displays a certain aggressiveness in her work. It seems that she carries the emotional burdens from home into her environment. Friends reflect to Marlene that they miss her joy and lightness, noting a perpetually somber expression on her face. Some even start avoiding her because she appears angry, further reinforcing Marlene's sense of disconnection and prevailing loneliness.

Furthermore, Marlene always seems to be only partially present. Her thoughts are always consumed by her mother, worrying about her and planning what she should cook for her in the evening in order to please her. When she feels anger, she tries to suppress it until she returns home to visit her mother. Consequently, it becomes challenging for her to fully engage with her friends and colleagues and to be fully present in her environment.

Example 2: Liane in codependency with her alcoholic husband.

The first few years of Liane and Peter's marriage were filled with happiness. However, after the birth of their first child and Liane's decision to stay at home, problems began to arise. When Peter would come home in the evenings after a long day at work, Liane longed for togetherness and loving conversation. Unfortunately, Peter would often be tired, irritable, and withdrawn. This left Liane feeling extremely frustrated and fearful, questioning whether she was still loved or had lost her attractiveness. In response to this fear, Liane started to protect herself internally by becoming moody and critical and secretly blaming Peter for her own unhappiness.

Peter started spending increasingly longer hours at work, and over time, Liane noticed the smell of alcohol on him. When she confronted him about it, Peter immediately became defensive and criticized her, silencing her by forcefully placing his hand over her mouth. He would then slam the door and stay out for an extra hour the next day. This phase was marked by intense arguments between the two, with Liane screaming and accusing Peter of destroying their marriage, only to take the blame minutes later and apologize.

As time went on, Liane became increasingly concerned about the growing number of incidents. One afternoon, an employee from Peter's company called looking for him as he had not shown up for work. Poor performance and warnings followed. Liane found herself making more and more excuses for Peter's absence at work, fabricating explanations and sharing stories of his illness with friends in an effort to evoke sympathy rather than anger. Meanwhile, Peter's drinking worsened, and he became increasingly unresponsive.

It was only when Liane approached her husband with tears and without aggression that he seemed to soften. He would apologize, bring her flowers, and go to work. On days like these, Liane would experience hope and rejoice. However, as soon as she expressed her own will or fears, Peter would become stubborn again and reach for the bottle. He would accuse Liane of meddling and deflect any responsibility.

The situation reached a breaking point when, following an argument, Peter disappeared for the weekend and spent the night at another woman's house after a binge at his local pub. Liane was overcome with jealousy but also torn by guilt over the argument and consumed by fear. For the first time, she openly confronted Peter about his alcohol addiction. Peter stared at her, raised his hand, but then abruptly left the room. Trembling in the kitchen, Liane realized that she had reached a dead end.

Question 1: How can codependency be identified in Liane's behavior?

Liane internalizes Peter's aggressive and dismissive behavior, believing that she is at fault and searching for her own flaws that may lead him to reject her. She sees his problem as something directly related to her, personally involving herself and reacting in a dismissive manner as a means of self-protection.

As Peter's drinking becomes regular, Liane takes on the role of protecting and managing his responsibilities. She makes excuses for him at work, fabricates explanations, and even lies on his behalf.

When she discovers that she can mitigate Peter's actions through gentleness and softness, she seizes this opportunity, albeit unconsciously. She wants to express her genuine pain and vulnerability, but she also uses this opportunity to exert control over his addictive behavior, aiming to keep herself safe.

Liane oscillates between confronting Peter and blaming herself, but whenever he becomes angry, she retreats. She is so enmeshed in her relationship with Peter that she fails to recognize his addiction as something separate from her own behavior. In Liane's perspective, Peter's addiction is intertwined with their love relationship. Despite Peter's lack of value for the relationship and his lack of control, even leading to infidelity, Liane remains fixated on finding fault within herself. It is only when Peter raises his hand in aggression after repeated transgressions that she begins to awaken to the reality of their situation.

Question 2: What internal motivation/trap might cause Liane to remain in codependency?

Liane's primary challenge stems from her low self-esteem and a self-destructive attitude, which manifest as boundary transgressions and a slight narcissistic tendency to relate everything to herself. She is disconnected from herself and constantly preoccupied with her partner. Despite this, she perceives herself as the central figure in all events, both negative and positive. Liane's behavior exhibits traits of codependency, particularly love addiction, as she becomes addicted to attention and affection. Her internal motivation is driven by a need for control, hoping to bind her partner to her and manipulate their behavior to fulfill her desires. However, she lacks the ability to establish healthy standards, set boundaries, and say no to anything that may harm her.

Question 3: How does Liane's own physical and emotional sensations manifest?

Physically, Liane often experiences a strong urge to pull her hair out. Internally, she berates herself with thoughts like, "Why am I so stupid? How could I say something like that?!" or "How could he do that? How could he?" She feels the urge to scream, wriggle, squirm, and shriek. However, her physical posture reflects a different reality; she often hunches forward with her head pulled between her shoulders. When she attempts to confront Peter, she instinctively pulls her head back to protect herself from a potential attack. She yearns to shed her skin and escape from tense situations, but instead, she feels trapped in a whirlwind of emotions that she cannot break free from.

Emotionally, Liane becomes entangled in the drama of the relationship. She senses a surge of strong love when the relationship is strained and experiences bouts of lovesickness. During arguments with Peter, she feels an intense love blossoming within her and repeatedly makes a promise to herself not to give up on him, to fight for their relationship. She heroically convinces herself that she will carry and save him, believing that she can be the woman he needs.

Question 4: How does the codependent relationship affect other areas of Liane's life?

In other relationships, Liane often struggles to be taken seriously. Her wavering opinions and lack of stability make her unreliable, and she tends to attribute failures to her husband or child. As a result, her friends and relatives may initially doubt her claims about Peter's alcoholism and aggressive behavior. Liane is disconnected from her center and fails to assert her boundaries, instead acting and communicating based on feigned emotions that conceal her true pain. Consequently, she gives off an impression of a slightly hysterical, exaggerated, and lonely wife who seeks attention. This attitude strains her relationships and perpetuates the root cause of her challenges: her lack of self-love and healthy boundaries, which hinder genuine connections with others.

Furthermore, Liane's relationship with Peter indirectly affects other areas of her life. She struggles to engage in topics unrelated to her personal drama, making it difficult for her to find a receptive ear and open heart among her friends. The prevailing atmosphere of suffering dominates conversations, causing friends and acquaintances to withdraw when they realize that the attention initially given to Liane is not reciprocated.

Example 3: Tina, in a codependent relationship with her depressed partner

Tina may appear to have both feet firmly planted in life, being a successful student working on her bachelor's thesis, living in a big city, and having a solid circle of friends. However, upon closer observation, certain inconsistencies emerge behind the stable facade of Tina's life. While she possesses a strong character, a firm voice, and exhibits political engagement, along with a bright mind and broad general knowledge, she struggles to complete her bachelor's thesis and often finds herself unable to overcome her own barriers. Periodically, she withdraws from social interactions for weeks, maintaining contact with only one person—her partner, Daniel. They live hours apart and see each other only twice a month for a few days. During their time together, they often spend it in bed, watching movies, consuming alcohol, and Daniel smoking marijuana. Even after Daniel leaves, Tina continues to display procrastinating and passive behavior for some time.

How do Tina's seemingly different behaviors reconcile? What leads a strong and self-reliant individual, highly valued and respected by her friends, to repeatedly fall into a severely depressive world alongside her partner?

The time Tina and Daniel spend together is accompanied by a profound heaviness. Tina recognizes that both she and Daniel are deeply depressed, yet she consciously chooses not to question the partnership because of it. A glimpse into their childhoods reveals deep traumas for both of them. Tina's past is marked by abuse, while Daniel experienced a tumultuous journey to America. These traumatic experiences suppress Tina's vibrant and life-affirming side, activating her inner child, which resonates with Daniel—a partner whose behavior is primarily passive and depressive. Tina's values of not devaluing others for their wounds, along with her strong empathy, reinforce the dynamic that unfolds as a downward spiral between the two individuals. Tina and Daniel perceive themselves as a conspiratorial couple against the world, retreating into their own small, protected realm, despite not overtly viewing their environment as hostile and possessing intellectual capabilities. They avoid arguments, and conflict topics that would typically stir emotions in others do not affect them. Their unity appears to be an unspoken rule.

Tina faces a significant challenge when Daniel starts asking her for money. This situation conflicts with her desire for independence and a self-reliant partner. However, acknowledging these feelings would call the relationship into question and force Tina to confront her patterns, not only becoming aware of her trauma but also engaging in intensive healing work. In an attempt to evade the issue, she repeatedly distracts herself, straddling between two positions without taking a firm stance. It is not until she realizes that Daniel has become increasingly passive and withdraws from her that she feels the pressure mounting. Questions arise within her: Will I only receive love if I provide money? Must I always exceed my limits in the relationship as well to ensure our bond?

Question 1: How can codependency be identified in Tina's behavior?

The most noticeable aspect is that Tina seems to diminish her strong personality whenever her partner is present, even during phone conversations. A friend observes that Tina speaks to Daniel in a reserved manner as if she's cautious not to assert herself fully. When confronted about it, Tina admits, "Yes, something in me is afraid of upsetting Daniel. I fear his aggression if he feels overwhelmed by me. We fear each other, I believe. Our depression makes us feel safe together. We both fear strength because we confuse it with crossing boundaries."

Tina is aware of what is happening and often acknowledges her codependent tendencies to her friends. She explains, "Not only have I experienced abuse myself, but my mother and sister suffered as well. So I feel the need to protect them. I pay more attention to others, currently Daniel than to myself. This keeps me dependent on Daniel's lifestyle, his passivity, his detachment from the world, his marijuana addiction. I am codependent because I can always understand everyone."

Question 2: What internal motivation/trap might cause Tina to remain in codependency?

Tina's internal trap is rooted in her hidden fear. On the surface, she appears courageous, a feminist who fights for justice. She is independent, educated, and serves as a role model to many. However, deep inside, she is filled with panic when faced with anything representing strength or power. When Daniel exploits his passivity as leverage, Tina's underlying sense of smallness becomes apparent. She fears being overwhelmed if she doesn't comply with his wishes. Daniel is her first and only partner at the age of thirty, and she is afraid of any power that comes too close, particularly when it originates from men. Tina feels comfortable and safe with strong women. Despite being aware of the origins and patterns of her circumstances, Tina's inner motivation within the codependent structure is to procrastinate. She explains to her friends, "I know all of this, but I simply lack the strength to address it. I should be allowed to just be depressed. Yes, I'm miserable, but I'm okay with it. At least I'm safe. That's what matters most."

Tina prioritizes the feeling of security above all other desires. Her wounded inner self has no concept of what it feels like to be simultaneously happy, connected, mentally healthy, and safe. Consequently, she enters into a codependent relationship with a man who appears safe to her, albeit without providing her with a mentally healthy environment.

Question 3: How do Tina's own physical and emotional sensations manifest?

Tina practices self-acceptance, but her mental wavering between two aspects of her personality is also reflected in her body image: she experiences fluctuating weight gain and loss. Her skin may be affected by pimples due to an unhealthy diet and smoking, yet Tina takes care to dress beautifully, apply makeup, and strive to feel at home in her body. Her body serves as a fortress that offers protection while also being the site of past pain and boundary violations. Thus, she alternates between feeling very comfortable and extremely uncomfortable. Physical intimacy with Daniel is only possible for Tina after they have retreated to her bed for hours, creating a castle-like environment where they repeatedly communicate their shared trauma. In those moments, Tina seeks refuge in Daniel's touch, finding a sense of security under its protective cover, and she acts relatively uninhibited. She attempts to conceal the discomfort and vulnerability that exist alongside intimacy.

Question 4: How does the codependent relationship affect other areas of Tina's life?

Tina's friendships remain stable, but they are occasionally strained by her tendency to withdraw and disconnect. Tina's friends also grapple with significant psychological challenges, although in different areas. They navigate their emotions respectfully, avoiding burdening one another, and their interactions are understanding and empathetic. Tina's friends struggle, particularly when it comes to withholding their opinions about her relationship and allowing Tina to make her own choices. They find it difficult to comprehend why Tina chooses a partner whom they perceive as beneath her level and allows her potential to be inhibited by his depression. They hope that one day Tina will utilize her immense potential to take a new direction in life.

The primary effect of Tina's codependency is that making plans with her becomes unreliable. She frequently disappears suddenly into her castle with Daniel, cutting herself off from her environment.

> **Inspiration**
>
> **Self-Reflection**
>
> If you suspect that you are exhibiting codependent patterns in a relationship, try to describe the situation you are in from the perspective of an impartial observer. Put yourself in the shoes of a stranger who is observing your relationship and behavior in a non-judgmental manner. Alternatively, you can choose a person who is sympathetic to you and with whom you have positive feelings.
>
> Take a moment to reflect on what is happening and how the other person perceives you. You can do this through a soliloquy or by writing down your thoughts. Answer the four questions that have been presented in the previous examples, while also including your personal assessment and reflecting on your inner motivations. Approach this exercise as a purely observational practice, where you examine the current state of your relationship and try to understand its background. The goal is not to find an immediate solution, but rather to gain a deeper understanding of your situation.

Afterward, consider writing yourself a letter with comforting words, as if you were a good friend offering support. Encourage yourself to continue on your healing path and to not lose hope. Sometimes, it can be beneficial to confide in someone and share your feelings and situation instead of keeping everything to yourself. Are there people who truly understand what your relationship is like? Do you have confidants who can provide both understanding and honest feedback, or who are simply willing to listen? Particularly in cases of codependency, it is wise to involve people you trust and who have a firm grasp on their own lives. If you often find yourself trapped in internal confusion and struggle to objectively evaluate your situation, or if you feel manipulated and unable to act from a place of strength, supportive and honest friends can assist you in your journey.

Self-Love Reflection

Take some time to embark on a reflective journey, both into your past and your present environment. Recall moments when other people have expressed words or acts of loving care that made you feel:

"I am important. I am valuable. This person sees me."

If you'd like, you can write down how this loving attitude has permeated your being and left a lasting impact, evoking a warm feeling within you. Can you sense how these small gestures continue to inspire and encourage you on your journey today? Which aspects of your being do they highlight that you particularly appreciate?

Chapter 4
Codependence in Relationships

"Our dependency makes slaves out of us, especially if this dependency is a dependency of our self-esteem."

Fritz Perls

Codependent patterns are particularly common in the realm of love relationships. What could be the underlying reason for this?

For most individuals, a love relationship represents a significant stage—a stage where the pages of old dramas are pulled out from dusty drawers, and the familiar play of pain is reenacted. The hope is that this time, the crucial scenes will be reinterpreted, and a different experience will unfold.

Our subconscious mind exerts significant influence, directing over ninety percent of our behaviors, feelings, and attitudes toward life. Even the choice of our partner tends to fall within the realm of the subconscious. When we encounter someone new whom we feel drawn to, our emotions tell us, "There is a closeness in this connection that feels familiar, as if I've known this person since time immemorial! They must be the right one."

Due to the familiarity of the reality we co-create with our partner, we fall in love and believe that we have found our place. However, it is only later that we realize, "This person is just like my mother/father! How did this happen? Wasn't I looking for someone different from my parents? I wanted to live differently than before!"

Deep inside us, the barometer of mate choice aligns with the desire to transform drama into romance. We yearn for our story to have a positive ending, for the conflicts to be resolved, and for the points of pain to be released. Specifically, this means that if our father was cold, dismissive, or aggressive, we might seek a partner who can manage and overcome their aggression out of love for us—unknowingly drawn to someone struggling with (initially concealed) aggression.

Similarly, if our mother was sick and unable to take care of us, we long for a partner who would go out of their way to care for us at all times, often gravitating towards someone who also struggles with prioritizing our needs over their own. Many codependents describe this longing, saying, "I have yearned to be important enough to someone that they would overcome their own obstacles and prove their love for me. I desire to feel valued by having someone wholeheartedly dedicate themselves to me and become the best version of themselves."

However, in doing so, we often choose partners who have their own challenges and lack a healthy, foundational emotional structure, mirroring the unresolved pain we have not yet taken responsibility for. We enter the relationship with the intention to heal but inadvertently resurrect the old, painful dynamics with our current partner. Unless both individuals are attentive and self-aware, they miss the opportunity to heal together and learn how to cultivate a healthy relationship. Instead, they expect the other person to heal their wounds while neglecting to take responsibility for their own growth. Thus, the cycle of pain from their inner child repeats, reinforcing their negative self-perception inherited from childhood: "You are not valuable (enough)."

Fundamentally, a partnership serves as a vehicle for old pain to resurface and reveal itself. We find ourselves confronted with our defense mechanisms, projections onto our partner, and the inner image of an enemy we project onto them. In the context of the partnership, we experience echoes of our powerlessness, anger, helplessness, insecurity, and dependency—reminiscent of our childhood experiences, where we believed that nothing would ever change. Unless we awaken and become aware of the dynamics at play in our subconscious, this pattern may persist. We may break up and seek out a new partner, but the old drama will continue to unfold until we address the underlying patterns that influence our choice of partners.

Therefore, the ideal scenario involves a combination of mindful partnering and a shared commitment to view any emerging issues as opportunities for joint healing. When both individuals in the relationship are aware of the presence of codependent patterns and approach them with wisdom and insight, they can work together to transform these patterns while taking personal responsibility.

The challenge lies in the fact that codependency often goes unnoticed until it has already taken hold. It is typically the codependent partner who unconsciously selects a person who fits into this dynamic—a partner on whom they become dependent and who lacks a solid sense of self. Initially, the codependent partner may perceive the early stages of the relationship as close, trusting, and romantic. They are empathetic and understanding, believing that they have finally found love. However, it is only when old, painful emotions resurface and they experience disappointment that they begin to recognize and realize, "I've seen this before. It's the same old pattern. It feels familiar because it's what I've always known. I attracted a narcissistic partner who didn't prioritize my genuine needs; instead, they were focused solely on themselves. And I mistakenly thought it was romantic to 'wait for them to be ready to love.' What was I thinking?"

The following dynamics are commonly observed in codependent relationships within a partnership:

1. I (as a codependent) adapt my behavior to the other person to maintain loyalty and seek symbiosis.

I struggle with being alone in my own stance, opinions, and worldview. The discomfort of relying solely on my judgment and making decisions based on my convictions without outside reassurance is overwhelming. When faced with opposing opinions from my partner, I immediately fear their rejection if I don't conform.

Conflict terrifies me, as any argument with a loved one triggers the fear of abandonment. I struggle to comprehend that disagreement can coexist with unity. Standing up for myself often means risking exclusion and choosing between honoring my inner truth and maintaining my place in the community. Throughout my life, I have never experienced being loyal to myself while still being fully accepted for who I am.

I lack a clear sense of self, and I hope my partner can provide that clarity. Behind my conformist behavior lies a constant question: "Who am I? Who do you want me to be?" I yearn for guidance and struggle to prioritize the stirrings of my heart, my desires, needs, and boundaries. I haven't learned to embrace them as valuable contributions to the creation of a healthy relationship. In the past, my wants and needs were often seen as burdens or annoyances, so I learned to adapt to fit societal expectations.

I fear loneliness, and I'm willing to sacrifice myself to avoid it. I would rather lose myself in the feeling of merging with another person than be completely autonomous but alone. The fear of rejection and exclusion is so overwhelming that I am compelled to avoid these experiences at all costs. Paradoxically, my willingness to sacrifice myself often provokes my partner's anger, reinforcing my feelings of inferiority. I frequently hear my partner urging me to take a stand, but this demand leaves me feeling powerless and helpless because I struggle to identify what I truly want. Despite my efforts to fulfill their every wish, I seem to achieve the opposite. Breaking free from this destructive cycle feels like an insurmountable challenge.

2. I am codependent because I struggle to find stability and meaning in my own life – I seek external validation.

I have always felt insignificant and less important compared to others. Their lives seem more glamorous, exciting, and captivating, causing me to divert my attention away from myself. I find solace in asking others about their lives and encouraging them to share their experiences while I remain in the background, avoiding the spotlight.

Deep down, I obsessively search for something that will ignite my passion. I long to find something that fully engages me, allows me to rediscover myself, and helps me thrive. However, whenever I feel a lasting enthusiasm for something, it seems that someone else has already found their niche in that area, causing my interest to wane. I feel compelled to find something extraordinary, something that sets me apart. Consequently, I remain on the sidelines, waiting for the perfect opportunity.

This waiting game also extends into my relationship. My partner pursues their dreams, and I cheer them on from the sidelines. I become the reliable support system that keeps everything running smoothly. In this dynamic, my partner becomes the project through which I find purpose. Neglecting my own needs, I immerse myself in my partner's life, living in their shadow. I am there to lift their spirits when they are down, believing that they couldn't thrive without me. This dynamic helps me keep my anxiety in check, providing me with a sense of power and helping me escape feelings of insignificance.

Deep down, I have ambitions of my own, but I am plagued by a fear of failure. The thought of risking everything and potentially embarrassing myself, especially in my own eyes, is terrifying. What if the grand idea I have of myself is nothing more than an illusion? Therefore, I choose to remain in the background, accepting mediocrity. I am codependent on my partner because it allows me to anchor the theoretical meaning and stability of life in the connection with them without risking personal failure.

3. I am codependent because I struggle to sincerely trust others – I seek control.

To be honest, I have always been drawn to those who are weak and in need of help. I've believed for the longest time that I possessed an exceptionally compassionate heart. However, I have come to realize that my desire to help stems from a fear of not being wanted by healthy and ambitious individuals. I find it difficult to trust—neither life itself, the people around me, nor even myself. If I discover that the true motivation behind my helpfulness is not entirely selfless, how can I trust others to be genuine with me? Will their presence be driven solely by pity? What could possibly motivate someone else to love me? Who am I, really?

The fear of losing inner control and questioning everything I know is so overwhelming that I would rather focus on supporting someone in need. In doing so, I can be certain that I won't be rejected. I become indispensable—after all, who else would willingly make such sacrifices?

Trust necessitates the belief that life has good intentions for me. Sadly, I lack that certainty. I thus prefer to remain in a realm that I can control. In a partnership, particularly with a healthy and self-assured individual, control becomes nearly impossible. They choose to be with me because they genuinely want to, not because they feel obligated to. The thought of this is unimaginably terrifying. What if someone were to leave me simply because they no longer desired me? Enduring such a scenario would be far worse than having someone around who depends on me.

The fear of not being loved unconditionally stems from my deep-seated sense of inferiority. I question whether I am truly deserving of such love. No one has ever cherished me just as I am—and truth be told, I haven't fully embraced myself either. While trust is a familiar concept to me, and I often discuss it, I am unfamiliar with how it truly feels. I constantly keep a backdoor open in my relationships. In fact, when I encounter someone who demonstrates a certain level of self-assertiveness, I am prone to behaving unreasonably to prove that their will alone is insufficient to earn my love. I feel the need to validate my own mistrust. I tend to disrupt moments of harmony, as hidden clouds seem to lurk behind every peaceful facade.

Inspiration

Write a text about your codependent behavior, similar to the example above, if you recognize it within yourself. Adopt a writing style that acknowledges the validity of these feelings, the presence of past wounds, and the desire to take inventory of them now.

It's important to remember that everything is allowed to be—it already exists within you. The more openly you can acknowledge your actions and the motivations behind them, the sooner you can accept yourself in this area and begin to change certain patterns.

Codependency in Relationships

> Above all, it's crucial that you meet yourself as you truly are in this moment. Remind yourself that you are not defined by your behavior alone. Within you lies a deeper essence, a core that goes beyond the choices you had to make in order to survive as a child. Embrace yourself, including all your neuroses, and offer yourself comfort and encouragement. In the next chapter, we will explore the process of lovingly letting go of old patterns that no longer serve you.

Self-Love Reflection

Adapted from the previous self-love exercise:

Take a moment to write down what you genuinely appreciate about yourself. Reflect on the external and internal qualities that bring warmth to your heart. What aspects of yourself would you like to embrace today and offer a loving, heartfelt smile?

If you'd like, write yourself a card filled with words of love and kindness. You can choose to send it a few weeks or days later, creating a beautiful surprise for yourself. You may even develop a habit of this exercise, receiving a monthly card that serves as a source of encouragement. It's possible that exactly four weeks later, you'll find yourself in need of the uplifting words that flowed from your pen before.

Chapter 5
Breaking Free from Codependence

Moving away from codependency may feel like an immense mountain standing in front of you after exploring the previous chapters. How is it possible not only to recognize these deep-rooted patterns but also to resolve them and create different experiences in the future?

Embarking on the path of healing requires courage and a willingness to leave behind familiar but draining paths. Perhaps you have endured exhausting experiences and find yourself physically, mentally, and spiritually depleted. Recognizing the need for growth, you sense the call for a new, uncharted horizon. It necessitates a period of recovery, rest, and creating space for healing to take place. Along this journey, you will have experiences with yourself and others that allow you to establish a healthy foundation within your relationship with yourself.

Codependency drains our energy because it sidesteps essential steps of personal growth. We inherently yearn for growth, and when we inhibit this natural process, we become depleted, feeling increasingly drained. This dynamic can take a toll on our well-being.

Therefore, it is time to provide an overview of the steps that will guide you toward the desired path of freedom, self-reliance, and healing expression within yourself and your relationships. Remember, the path is formed as you walk it, and this chapter serves as a map to help you navigate in the right direction.

To embark on this path to freedom, an important prerequisite is self-awareness: acknowledging that your current situation is no longer sustainable and that you desire a change. Making a resolute decision without leaving any back doors open will assist you in persevering through challenging phases without giving up.

It is important to note that not everyone can make this decision overnight and immediately change everything in one attempt. Most often, it takes time, patience, and small steps, and that is perfectly fine—there is no need to worry. As some behavioral therapists suggest, we remain in an unhealthy situation until we have truly had enough. It is at this point that the decision becomes easier, fueled by intrinsic motivation, as the benefits of staying in the current state no longer outweigh the suffering. The change becomes a necessity once we have reached the point of no return.

If you are codependent, you might have believed that you reached this turning point on multiple occasions, only to find yourself falling back into old patterns. This phenomenon is characteristic of codependence. However, the difference between this and a genuine turning point is the strength you feel within yourself—an inner boundary you are no longer willing to cross in order to preserve the relationship.

Continuously seek and reaffirm this boundary within yourself on the path to freedom. Remind yourself of it frequently and become aware that the time has come to stand up for yourself.

The Main Fears of Codependents in the Healing Process

During the journey of recovery, codependents often face several main fears that can be challenging to overcome. When reaching out for help, many individuals are already at their breaking point. The prospect of breaking free from the cycle of codependency without the assurance of feeling genuinely fulfilled and happy without the other person can seem like an insurmountable mountain. It is in this space that relapses frequently occur, leaving friends and relatives silently bewildered, questioning how the codependent can endure such a situation any longer.

The Fear of Being Alone

The end of a codependent relationship usually signifies a phase of solitude or being single for the codependent individual. Suddenly, their previous primary task of caring for the other person disappears, and they are thrust back onto themselves. This newfound freedom initially feels unsettling, as their thoughts used to revolve entirely around the other person. It creates an empty space that is not immediately filled with a new purpose. This emptiness can be overwhelming, leading to various concerns:

- What should I do with my time?
- I am now confronted with my own feelings and discomfort. I fear the emotions and pain that might arise.
- Who am I?
- What if I will be alone forever?

The fear of being alone is so distressing for many because they struggle to envision it as only a temporary phase. Although this phase is crucial and often inevitable, it can resemble a dark tunnel that must be traversed before glimpses of light can be seen at its end.

It is necessary to confront everything that has been avoided throughout the years of codependency. Our inner pain will continue to haunt us until we are ready to face it. If you have made the decision to break free but find yourself relapsing into a new similar relationship or keeping the old contact alive, you are essentially trapped in a cycle. The opportunity to confront the fear of being alone will always resurface.

To address the fear of being alone, consider the following thoughts:

- I understand that this phase is essential for my healing journey. It is a gift I give myself.
- Being alone does not mean being alone forever. In fact, it is through this phase that a genuine community can be cultivated.

- I have also experienced feelings of loneliness even when I was with someone. Now is the time to direct my energy inward.
- Self-imposed solitude should not be equated with the deep-rooted fear of rejection. By consciously choosing to be alone, I am not rejecting others. Instead, I am embracing a phase of self-love and personal recovery.

The Fear of the Crash

Codependency provides a sense of security and stability for those affected by it. The constant focus on the needs of the dependent individual and their own connection to them leaves little time for contemplating how to shape their lives independently and according to their true needs. However, when the end of a codependent relationship looms, a daunting mountain of inner tasks emerges:

- Understanding one's own needs
- Establishing healthy boundaries
- Cultivating personal stability and resilience
- Developing assertiveness and willpower
- Nurturing cooperation with others without losing one's own center

This prompts questions about one's relational capacity and areas for self-improvement. How have I contributed to this situation? Where can I work on myself? An emotional crash can also occur when one realizes the profound transformation of previously assumed roles that come with the end of a codependent relationship.

Suddenly, the old patterns are questioned. Have I taken less responsibility than I believed? What does it mean to fully embrace the part of myself that played a role in creating the situation? How can I learn to truly love and accept myself unconditionally, with all my strengths and weaknesses? What weaknesses do I see in the other person that I may also sense in myself but struggle to fully accept? How can I let these weaknesses coexist within me without attempting to control or burden the other person and instead foster deep intimacy with my own shadows?

Another significant fear is the void left without the presence of the other person. Ending a codependent relationship does not immediately resolve the internal struggles. It is only at this point that many individuals realize the depth of their entanglement and how profoundly they have been immersed in the quagmire of codependency. They had internal defenses, downplayed the situation, and utilized various coping mechanisms to escape the pain of the breakup. It is during this phase that the dependent emotional structure becomes fully exposed.

Some codependent individuals report experiencing strong withdrawal symptoms after a breakup, particularly in romantic relationships. This revelation highlights that codependency itself is an addiction with its own patterns of dependency.

The Fear of One's Own History
Upon realizing their own contribution to the codependent situation, a space for introspection opens up. Through self-reflection, various stories from the past come to light, shedding light on the factors that contributed to the development of codependent patterns. It is through delving into our past that we can truly bring about change, understanding ourselves better, and accepting ourselves with love. This process also reveals where new paths must be taken in order to have different experiences in the future.

For many individuals, their own history remains shrouded in darkness for a significant period of time. The realization of the extent to which their behavior has been unconsciously driven can be daunting. Many codependents describe a collapse of their self-image during the liberation process.

Previously, they believed they were exceptionally empathetic, loving, self-sacrificing, and helpful, which bolstered their self-esteem. However, they now come to understand that these attributes were survival strategies they adopted as children to cope with an unsafe environment. They can no longer rely on these attributes to boost their self-esteem or give them a sense of power. Instead, they recognize that these attributes were merely a crutch they held onto throughout their lives.

Embarking on a journey into the past requires courage. It takes courage to confront one's own issues unconditionally and acknowledge them. It is not always about blaming others for our unhappiness. Like everyone else, we carry pain within us, and often our actions stem from that pain. Only we ourselves can face this pain and initiate the process of change. No one else can undertake this journey on our behalf.

What is the Right Thing to Do?

The aim here is to break the cycle of anger and submission, which drains your energy and leaves you feeling tossed back and forth while losing sight of your own perspective. Neither anger nor submission can help you reconnect with yourself, especially if they serve to position you solely in relation to the other person.

The key question that can guide you out of this vicious cycle is: What is the RIGHT thing to do?

Doing the right thing means taking an action that is independent of your emotions, with a focus on your own healing and the resolution of the codependent situation. Your emotions are unlikely to assist you at this stage, as they still stem from the old patterns of codependency. You may rebel against the enmeshed connection, but as soon as you take a step out, fear takes hold, and you snap back into submission.

Imagine that the realm of your emotions exists in a separate inner space from the space where you make decisions. Your emotions are valid and deserve attention, but they should not dictate the right decision you make.

This step is not easy, and you may need to practice frequently in order to separate your emotions from reason-based decision-making. It may be helpful to remind yourself that reason also arises from love. When you make a decision that feels painful but is ultimately beneficial for your well-being, it is an act of self-love. In the future, your decisions will be accompanied by emotions, but they will no longer stem from dependence. Instead, they will support you in staying true to yourself.

Marina recognized that she had reached the point of no return. While her partner, in a drunken state, continued to unleash his narcissistic rage over the phone, humiliating her with his words, something significant occurred: Marina observed herself unable to end the call. The months of emotional turmoil flashed before her eyes as she recalled numerous instances where she went to great lengths to shield her partner from the consequences of his behavior. She lied on his behalf, made excuses to his employer, concealed their problems from friends, and even retrieved him from late-night pub visits to prevent potential accidents on his way home. In that moment, Marina saw herself fully illuminated amidst the chaos, and she realized that neither her anger towards her partner nor her willingness to sacrifice could ever bring about lasting change in his behavior.

In a remarkable turn of events, Marina did something she had never been able to do before. Slowly, she removed the phone from her ear, still filled with her partner's shouts and rants. Her heart raced in her chest as she took a deep breath. And then, with newfound courage, she hung up the call.

This particular moment in Marina's life signifies a point of no return, followed by a significant action. Previously, she had found herself crying on the phone, apologizing, listening empathetically, and attempting to de-escalate the situation through communication. However, this time, she took a genuine and tangible step forward.

This small yet transformative experience will soon be followed by other challenging situations, where Marina will have to make choices that align with what is right, despite her emotions. Her heart may race, and her mind might try to recreate the familiar dynamics of the past. Perhaps, just three minutes later, she will feel tempted to call her partner back, succumbing to a sense of submission. However, Marina now has the power to resist this temptation by not allowing her emotions to control her and by tending to her own pain.

Had Marina hung up in anger, driven solely by her emotions, it would have been an act of rebellion. But this time, her action was preceded by a profound realization and a deliberate decision. As a result, Marina can now utilize this pivotal moment to gradually liberate herself from the grip of codependency, one step at a time.

Inspiration

If you have not yet reached the point of no return, it is not necessary to wait for it. You can still make the right decision without that inner push. Mediation can be a helpful tool in this process.

To do this, envision in a meditative state how your future will unfold if you continue along the same path. Start with the understanding that you cannot change the other person, as it is a natural law. Your persistence will not bring about change in them.

Next, imagine how your life can transform once you free yourself from this dependency. Feel the sense of relief wash over you as new possibilities emerge. Envision the weight being lifted off your shoulders. Picture yourself looking back on this moment twenty years from now, knowing that this decision paved the way for the wonderful life you are leading today.

Tips and Tricks

- Seek role models: Look for individuals in your surroundings or seek out inspiring mentors, coaches, and role models who have mastered the art of doing what is right without feeling inadequate. Recognize that they prioritize their own well-being in a healthy manner. Engage in conversations with these individuals or listen to their insights to learn how they have integrated self-love into their lives.

- Value yourself: Choose to be someone who consistently acts in alignment with what is right, and surround yourself with people who also follow their inner truth. This way, you can foster relationships with individuals whom you can rely on.

- Think long-term: An ancient saying from indigenous peoples advises us to consider the consequences of our actions a hundred years into the future. By doing so, we participate in shaping a positive future for our descendants. By making wise decisions today, you can create a healthy future for yourself as well.

What Do I Really Want?

This question addresses the state of confusion from which you must find your way out. The inquiry into what you truly desire arises from an inner space beyond your suffering and entanglement. Amidst the complexity of this emotional drama, it is difficult to freely sense your genuine aspirations. However, when you step back and view the situation from an external perspective, it becomes easier to discern how you actually wish to live.

Try the following exercise:

- "I was going to... instead, I'm just living..."
- "I actually wanted to... instead, I feel..."
- "I was going to... instead, I'm giving my time to..."
- ...

Repeat this exercise as often as you like. Objectively acknowledge that despite all the sacrifices, attempts, helpfulness, and even the illusion of control you may have, your current circumstances do not align with your true desires for a fulfilled life.

"What do I really want?"—this is a profound question that transcends superficiality. It cannot be answered by possessions, fleeting satisfaction, or feeding our neuroses. Instead, it leads us to explore the depth of a meaningful life. In the context of codependency, this question is crucial because it enables you to see beyond your current drama and realize that there is a life outside your present limitations waiting to be embraced. It ignites your longing for freedom, fulfillment, meaningful pursuits, and fertile ground on which your passion can flourish, catalyzing positive change for yourself and others. By recognizing the frustration in your current situation, you can reach for future possibilities that bring joy to your life. Such positive feelings are essential for initiating a transformative shift, as your genuine desires possess remarkable power to motivate you in the long run. To effect change, you require the surge of adrenaline and dopamine. These hormones are released through enthusiasm and positive experiences, accompanying you on your healing journey.

If you are not yet prepared to resolve your confusion by exploring what you truly want, you can revisit the step of making the right decision. A right decision brings inner peace, granting you the capacity to address this question. Between making the right decision and pondering your will, you will likely encounter feelings of despair or a sense of futility. These emotions are inherent to change, alongside a positive vision of the future. They represent the other side of the coin, signifying the need to confront your pain.

Liane has dedicated the past ten years to caring for her ailing mother, fully devoting herself and leaving little room for her own freedom. She constantly experiences feelings of guilt, believing she hasn't given enough and has abandoned her deeply unhappy and suffering mother. Now, Liane is attempting to break free from this guilt, but whenever she interacts with her mother, she finds herself torn and uncertain about whether she is permitted to live a self-reliant and independent life. She questions if she has the right to release herself from her mother's grip and focus on her own aspirations. Consequently, Liane frequently feels ungrateful, insignificant, and selfish.

However, with time, she learns to observe the emotions that keep her trapped in codependency from a distance. She recollects buried dreams and unfinished projects for which she never made time. This process is accompanied by a sense of melancholy and sadness as Liane recognizes how little love she has shown herself. In her caregiving role, she has neglected her own well-being, unintentionally mirroring the neglect she never wanted her mother to experience. From that point forward, reconnecting with her desires enables her to cultivate a renewed sense of self-love.

> **Inspiration**
>
> Keep a small wish journal where you can gather the desires that emerge from the depths of your heart. If you'd like, compare them with more superficial, instant gratification-oriented desires and sense the contrasting atmospheres they create. Pay attention to the type of desire that resonates with you on a deeper level and evokes a sense of authenticity. Which desires hold a profound significance and are worth aligning your life with? Is the longing for healthy relationships, free from codependency, one of those desires?

Tips and Tricks

- Cultivate introspection, particularly during moments when you find yourself losing your sense of self, prioritizing others' needs, and neglecting your own desires. Train yourself to create distance and dedicate time for reflection in these instances. Re-engage in conversations only after gaining clarity about your own will.

- Practice effective communication when experiencing confusion. Clearly express your desire for clarity and refrain from engaging in exhausting arguments. Manipulative conversations, where you are coerced into certain actions or burdened with guilt and shame, intensify feelings of confusion. Immediately discontinue such conversations and retreat to regain clarity. You may need to withdraw more frequently until you develop the ability to remain centered and regain a sense of purpose more readily.

- Pay attention to the contributions the other person brings to the relationship. Are you constantly setting up the buffet while they help themselves? Consider the "nourishment" you receive from them. Remember: They bring something to the table, but the crucial question is whether this "nourishment" truly satisfies your needs and promotes your well-being.

Who am I?

This question confronts the pattern of denial. A codependent relationship thrives when one disregards and denies one's own desire for integrity and truth. The process begins several steps earlier: many codependents are unaware of their true wants and their own identity. Consequently, they seek their identity in others or distract themselves with external activities, avoiding the question of who they truly are.

The inquiry into one's own identity goes beyond mere philosophical contemplation. Practical answers can be found that enable us to find our place in society and assume roles that align with our inner sense of self. To achieve this, we must delve deeply into our inner selves, cultivate stillness, and connect with our internal sensations. The question of who you are cannot be answered solely through external circumstances, no matter how well your life appears. Your circumstances provide insights into the state of your inner being, highlighting areas that require growth and healing. They assist you in the journey of self-discovery. However, your identity is something you can perceive within your inner core. It may elude verbal description, manifesting instead as a gut feeling, an awareness of your essential being. This essence is timeless and independent of external circumstances. Through this essence, you can discern whether your experiences are rooted in this inner source and align with it.

> **Inspiration**
>
> This exercise is commonly utilized in spiritual circles to delve deeper into the question of one's identity.
>
> To perform this exercise, engage with a partner. Sit facing each other. The task for the other person is to ask you, "Who are you?"
>
> Respond based on your initial instinct, without judgment.
> The other person continues to ask, "Who are you?"
> You provide an answer.
>
> This process allows you to delve beneath numerous layers and gain awareness of the "shells" you have constructed around the potential core response. Consider this exercise as a source of inspiration, connecting you with your inner self in the present moment.

Tips and Tricks

- The question serves multiple purposes, including the process of healthy detachment from others. Finding a definitive answer to who we truly are may be elusive, but we can establish a sense of inner belonging that reinforces our identity as a loved, independent being and helps us establish boundaries. Where does my personal space end and the other person's begin? Where have you intruded into someone else's domain and invested your energy in their responsibilities? Where do others cross your boundaries?

- Note: The answer to the question of who you are cannot be provided by anyone else. As you delve into your past, it's important to examine what others have taught you about your identity. Look at your current life from their perspective: Have you conformed to their perception of you? Does this sense of identity resonate with you?

- If you wish, imagine what the person you are in a codependent relationship with thinks about you. Reflect on your honest assumptions and consider whether the other person genuinely holds a healthy, respectful opinion of you and views you as an equal. If not, how does that perception make you feel? How do you desire others to perceive you? How do you want to perceive yourself?

Out of False Hope and Into Faith

False hope refers to the phase in which, as a codependent, you have already recognized the unhealthy direction the relationship has taken. You understand the role you have assumed and are aware that it does not bring you happiness. Despite this awareness, you continue to hold onto the hope that the other person will change. Even when there are fleeting moments of improvement or promises for a better future, you find yourself slipping back into the codependent position, no longer anchored in your own center.

Abandoning false hope entails placing complete trust in your instincts and intuition, which are well aware of the warning signs along your path. You make the decision to separate yourself from your emotions, do what is right for you, reclaim your energy, and embrace genuine faith.

What is the difference between hope and faith?

Genuine faith is built on trust in something that resonates deeply with your heart, aligns with your values, and reflects your inner truth. It involves connecting with another person in a way that feels liberating, where you can remain anchored in your own center. Genuine faith does not compromise your own boundaries but allows for an equal partnership, creating a reality that is healthy for both individuals. This may involve ending an unhealthy relationship and moving on. However, it can also mean that both parties acknowledge the issues and decide to seek help together. In such cases, it is crucial to assess whether the relationship has the potential to align with your desired vision. In other words, is it realistically possible to bridge the gap between reality and your aspirations?

Can my sick mother, who has never taken responsibility for me in thirty years, change her inner patterns in the near future to recognize me as an independent person and be there for me? Am I capable of freeing myself from my codependent patterns and viewing my mother as an equal? Are my expectations of myself and my mother realistic?

Is my narcissistic or dependent partner capable of making radical changes in their life? Do we both desire the same type of relationship and share the same goals? Is my partner truly committed to making the necessary efforts for positive change, evident through their actions?

In most cases, however, codependents must come to the realization that the healing they seek is not possible within their current relationship, at least not within the desired timeframe or in alignment with their inner truth. The reality is that a healing journey within a relationship with codependent tendencies requires a clear understanding of the actual circumstances and a willingness from both parties to embark on this path together. If the sole goal is to have a nice relationship in the near future, the current connection is unlikely to fulfill this.

- ♦ Evaluate your true desires for a healthy relationship.

- Above all, recognize what you are genuinely willing to invest. This point is of utmost importance as it will determine how you proceed in the process of breaking free from codependent patterns.

- Remember that simply removing the current person who matches your codependency tendencies from your life does not automatically heal your codependency. These two processes are only partially interconnected. True change and prevention of repeating past experiences with others can only be achieved when you reflect on and address your own issues independently.

- Embrace genuine faith in the healing process, having made an honest decision against false hope. By realistically assessing the circumstances and placing your faith in a change process that is grounded in reality, you can truly experience positive transformation.

Out of Credulity and into Trust

Genuine trust is developed over time with individuals or in circumstances that deserve that trust. It is an unhealthy misconception and a characteristic of codependence to give trust in situations where there is a high probability that it will not be reciprocated.

For example, giving pocket money to a drug-addicted son and trusting that he will use it responsibly, despite having previously spent it on drugs multiple times, will not lead to a satisfactory outcome. Similarly, it is unwise to repeatedly trust and open up to a husband who consistently belittles and takes advantage of your open attitude.

Trust should be given with caution and foresight. It is important to avoid projecting one's own past hurts or negative experiences onto a new connection and instead approach it with a trust that is based on its own merits and not influenced by external factors.

Healthy and enduring connections, whether in personal relationships, work environments, between couples, relatives, or parents and children, are built on trust that has been tested and supported by positive experiences.

- Cultivate an expectation that your trust will be rewarded with positive experiences.

- Positive experiences are essential for the development of a healthy, non-codependent relationship. This aspect is often overlooked, particularly by codependents who may remain trapped in false hope and may not even recognize genuine trust.

- Genuine trust feels liberating. Those who genuinely trust are relaxed, let go, radiate from within, and receive energy from the relationship.

Out of Altruism and into Genuine Devotion

Genuine devotion is built upon the foundation of deep trust and grounded faith in a realistic shared goal. With this solid groundwork, devotion can emerge as a heartfelt gift to the other person. It is no longer a pathway to being exploited or drained, but rather ignites and enriches the relationship, fostering equality, openness, and vulnerability.

You see, surrendering means being able to open up and reveal your true self to the other person. It is a sign of the healing process beginning. To surrender is to communicate the following to the other person:

"I reveal my authentic self, gradually unveiling my vulnerabilities. I trust that you genuinely care for me, that you appreciate me, and that we are both willing to invest in the relationship. I offer myself because I believe you provide a safe space."

Anyone who experiences this dynamic in any type of relationship is well on their way to breaking free from codependent patterns.

- Reflect on whether you have ever experienced true devotion and trust in a relationship. How did this devotion feel? What aspects were you certain of?

- How does the absence of devotion manifest in your current codependent tendencies? Are you excessively self-sacrificing, describing yourself as overly helpful, and always wanting to be there for others without considering your own needs? By doing so, can you sense how much you truly yearn to open up and wholeheartedly give of yourself?

- What do you need from your partner in order to fully reveal yourself and offer your genuine devotion? Are these expectations realistic, given the current circumstances?

- Embrace the potential for genuine surrender, even if it contrasts with your inclination towards self-sacrifice, as a crucial aspect when entering future relationships.

- In the context of parent-child relationships, devotion means that as a mother, father, or caregiver, you reclaim your role as a provider of security. You no longer subject yourself to unhealthy patterns. You heal, take responsibility, let go of feelings of guilt and shame, and cease blaming your child for any discomfort you may have experienced in your parental role. Courageously set boundaries and open yourself to love your child from the heart, which may also involve saying "no."

"Wise Advice"

In order to achieve a profound change in one's own life, as previously mentioned, role models are incredibly valuable. Many codependents have grown up in families where such role models were scarce. Their understanding of healthy relationships is often limited to what they have read in books, lacking personal experiences that foster positive self-esteem, as there are few individuals in their surroundings who genuinely embody it.

- If you decide to seek role models in your personal life outside of professional settings, remember this: Only those who truly live by their principles can provide competent guidance. Mere words are insufficient proof of being a good role model. A true role model is recognized through their actions, which naturally inspire others in the right direction, even without verbal instructions. Their life speaks volumes.

- It's also important to consider the attitudes and lifestyles of the individuals who accompany you on your journey out of codependency, both in conversations and as friends. If they carry similar emotional burdens and trigger points, unreflective discussions may result in surface-level exchanges driven by emotions without leading to genuine improvement. So, assess the purpose of your conversations: Are you engaging in dialogue to foster authentic, introspective change and provide comfort, or are you simply stirring up unresolved issues?

- Some codependents tend to seek agreement with their deeply entangled partner as a means to end the relationship together. They discuss with their partner and seek advice on what course of action to take. Initially, this approach may appear to be a peaceful and sensible request, but underlying codependent patterns come into play. The codependent individual struggles to make independent decisions, fearing rejection, separation, and the dissolution of the attachment. They may genuinely believe that separation would be beneficial for both parties, yet they seek agreement (which is rarely achievable) out of their dependent tendencies. It's crucial to avoid seeking advice from the person with whom you are entangled, even if they seem like a confidant during intimate moments.

Completion – When the Dependent Individual Becomes Unrecognizable

The journey of reaching a state of completion, marked by a sense of detachment, comes after navigating through challenging steps that simultaneously offer tremendous potential for personal growth. Let's summarize them once again:

- *Recognition:* Acknowledging that the current situation is unsustainable.
- *Decision:* Committing to change the circumstances.
- *Seeking support:* Turning to role models, seeking professional help, connecting with individuals who are invested in your personal growth.
- Emotion separation and fundamental decision-making - repeatedly.
- *Maintaining resilience:* Holding onto the belief in a realistic and healthy future.
- *Self-love:* Choosing relationships in which you can genuinely express and give yourself.

After weeks, possibly months, or even years have passed, you look back and reflect upon the deep emotional entanglement you once found yourself in. You consider the extent of energy you invested in that way of life and how it repeatedly left you feeling drained. Memories of tears, pleas, hope, and the desire to maintain control in an environment that felt profoundly unsafe resurface.

If your codependency was tied to an entangled relationship with a romantic partner, friend, or parent, you now find yourself asking, "How did I allow myself to become so dependent on this person? What initially attracted me to them? Why did I settle for far less than I deserved as a sensitive and valuable human being?"

In hindsight, it may be challenging to explain the intensity of infatuation that fueled the codependent bond. Nevertheless, you have successfully healed a part of yourself that no longer aligns with the unhealthy dynamics present in the other person.

"Today, I understand that I am deserving of relationships in which both giving and receiving are balanced. I am gradually learning to release the need to control others and anchor my self-esteem in their actions. Instead, I prioritize my own well-being, setting a healthy standard for how I expect to be treated in relationships.

I have outgrown codependency and moved forward. Although I acknowledge my propensity to be swept away by a desire for open surrender, I remain mindful of myself and continuously remind myself of my aspiration for relationships built on mutual respect and equality."

Self-Love Reflection

Engage in a form of self-reflection, regardless of your personal spiritual beliefs. You don't need to subscribe to a specific religion or have a particular connection to a higher power to engage in this practice. This self-love reflection is a way to lovingly connect with your inner self, cultivating mindfulness and tapping into a soulful place that empowers you.

In this reflection, express gratitude for your inherent worthiness of being acknowledged, supported, embraced, and loved. Affirm your trust in a future where you will experience this acknowledgment. Give thanks for the opportunity to grow in love, freedom, and healthy relationships.

Conclusion

Dependency and freedom are closely intertwined. True freedom can only be attained when we engage in voluntary connections with others that bring fulfillment to both parties and entail responsibilities. Only those who truly feel free within themselves can navigate these commitments in a healthy manner without losing their sense of self.

To achieve this inner freedom, it is crucial to establish deep roots and gradually gain certainty in our identity. Remember that the journey towards inner freedom starts from within, at the core of your being. When you feel overwhelmed and helpless, allow yourself to embrace these emotions, take deep breaths, and find stillness without feeling the need to take immediate action. Seek assistance whenever necessary, and recognize that you deserve to embark on the path away from codependency.

Beyond this pattern lies a space where you can rediscover yourself and create a life that provides genuine safety, security, and ample room for healthy growth.

Wishing you all the best on your journey!

Resources and Further Reading

Brown, B. (2010). *The gifts of imperfection: Let go of who you think you're supposed to be and embrace who you are.* Hazelden Publishing.

Fisher, B. (2004). *Rebuilding: When your relationship ends.* Impact Publishers.

Forward, S. (2019). *Emotional blackmail: When the people in your life use fear, obligation, and guilt to manipulate you.* HarperCollins.

Lancer, D. (2014). *Codependency for dummies.* Wiley.

Pia Mellody, J. M., Miller, A. W., & Miller, J. K. (2003). *Facing love addiction: Giving yourself the power to change the way you love.* HarperOne.

Rosenberg, M. (2003). *Nonviolent communication: A language of life.* PuddleDancer Press.

Simon, G. K. (2010). *In sheep's clothing: Understanding and dealing with manipulative people.* Parkhurst Brothers.

Stosny, S. (2008). *How to improve your marriage without talking about it*. Crown.

Van der Kolk, B. (2015). *The body keeps the score: Brain, mind, and body in the healing of trauma*. Penguin Books.

Zimbardo, P., & Boyd, J. (2009). *The time paradox: The new psychology of time that will change your life*. Simon and Schuster.

Top of Form

Bottom of Form

Made in the USA
Las Vegas, NV
26 March 2024

87770897R00075